The Stained-Glass Ceiling

The Stained-Glass Ceiling

Churches and
Their Women Pastors

Sally B. Purvis

Westminster John Knox Press
Louisville, Kentucky

Scripture quotations from the New Revised Standard Version of the Bible are copyright © 1989 by the Division of Christian Education of the National Council of the Churches of Christ in the U.S.A. and are used by permission.

Book design by Carol Eberhart

Cover design and photograph by Alec Bartsch

First edition

Published by Westminster John Knox Press
Louisville, Kentucky

This book is printed on acid-free paper that meets the American National Standards Institute Z39.48 standard. ∞

PRINTED IN THE UNITED STATES OF AMERICA

95 96 97 98 99 00 01 02 03 04 — 10 9 8 7 6 5 4 3 2 1

Library of Congress Cataloging-in-Publication Data

Purvis, Sally B.
    The stained-glass ceiling : churches and their women pastors / Sally B. Purvis. — 1st ed.
        p.   cm.
    Includes bibliographical references (p.).
    ISBN 0-664-25608-2 (alk. paper)
    1. Women clergy—Georgia—Atlanta—Case studies.   2. Women in the Anglican Communion—Georgia—Atlanta—Case studies.   3. Women in the Presbyterian Church—Georgia—Atlanta—Case studies.   I. Title.
    BV676.P87   1995
    262 .14 082—dc20   95-19608

Contents

Foreword

Leadership in the Christian church has taken different forms at various periods of history. In the beginning, those who knew Jesus and could share the story of his life, death, and resurrection were natural leaders. As time passed and the anticipated end of the age did not come, the needs of the fledgling church changed. Eventually persecutions and then establishment situations called for new patterns of Christian leadership.

In its evolution the church developed the practice of "ordaining" leadership—that is, setting apart a few people by prayer and laying on of hands to serve the needs of the wider community through sacramental acts and pastoral care. Understandings of ordination have varied over the centuries. In some instances ordained clergy have literally embodied a superhuman reality, something mysterious and otherworldly or ontologically different; at other times ordained clergy have been defined as ordinary persons tapped for special responsibilities by the larger community and empowered to ministries of word and sacrament, functionally, but not ontologically different from other forms of discipleship. Furthermore, in the practice of the church in western Europe, although women found important arenas for ministerial service, ordained ministry was understood to be a vocational option reserved for celibate men.

During the sixteenth-century Protestant Reformation, some of these assumptions changed. Martin Luther, as well as other Protestant clergy, married, arguing that clergy ought to have firsthand experience with family life. Later, as the global mission movement expanded in the eighteenth and nineteenth centuries, women took on leadership responsibilities historically reserved for ordained males. Soon the question of women's ordination began to haunt Protestant practice, especially in America.

First, laywomen within local congregations asked difficult questions: When is it acceptable for women to speak in church meetings? This was significant because in the early nineteenth century it was unseemly for women to address mixed groups, or "promiscuous assemblies." Next, Americans impressed with the democratic process wanted to know whether women could vote in church meetings or serve on the governing board, vestry, session, or council of a congregation. They also debated whether women could represent a local congregation at regional, diocesan, or national meetings. In most mainstream Protestant denominations no progress was made toward the ordination of women until women claimed significant power and influence as laity.

The Congregationalists, Baptists, and denominations with congregational polity resolved the issue of lay citizenship in the early nineteenth century. Once women were accepted as lay leaders, it was only a small step toward the ordination of women because these denominations do not require wider church approval to ordain anyone. The first woman ordained by a major Protestant denomination was Antoinette Brown. She was ordained by a small Congregational church in South Butler, New York, in 1853.

Denominations following presbyterial or episcopal polity moved much more slowly. With these denominations it was often necessary to develop a theological rationale justifying the election (or "ordination") of women as lay leaders (or elders) before the question of allowing women clergy could be addressed. Once they determined that no biblical or theological reason prevented women from speaking and ruling, these denominations moved to deal with women's ordination; however, the decision to ordain women to ministries of Word and sacrament was far from simple.

In fact, practical (not theological) questions kept these denominations from ordaining women well into the mid-twentieth century. Even after everyone agreed that no biblical or theological reasons existed that would prevent ordination of women, church leaders debated practical questions: Could a married woman do it? What would be the relationship of ordained ministry to mission and educational work? What if local church leaders did not want women pastors? Could a woman manage a large congregation? Could a woman be a bishop? Cautious leadership, male and female, ordained and lay, hesitated to ordain women if it might prove impractical.

Women, however, expanded their involvement in local church life, providing hospitality and unofficial leadership in many local settings. Women functioned as itinerant evangelists, moving around the countryside "witnessing" and "sharing" their faith—"planting" new churches. Women kept local congregations together following the untimely deaths of their pastor husbands. Women did what needed to be done, or what seemed blessed by the Holy Spirit, and nobody objected. As the years went by, most mainline American Protestant denominations found ways to overcome the practical barriers that kept them from ordaining women.

This book is a focused examination of the leadership of two women pastors in two mainline Protestant congregations in the late twentieth century. It recognizes that the leadership of women pastors in congregations within the Episcopal Church and the Presbyterian Church (U.S.A), especially in its southern congregations, is a relatively recent development.

The Protestant Episcopal Church in the United States stands in communion with worldwide Anglicanism and defines ordination and priestly orders within the framework of "apostolic succession." Furthermore, the issue of women's orders among Anglicans goes back to 1862, when the Bishop of London "ordered" a deaconess by "laying on hands." In the 1880s American Episcopalians began "setting apart" women as deaconesses, but it remained unclear exactly how the ordering of deaconesses related to the priesthood.

In 1964, the General Convention of the Episcopal Church in the U.S. asserted that deaconesses were "ordered" rather than "appointed." Almost a decade later, in 1972, the House of Bishops voted in favor of the principle of women's ordination to the priesthood, but a year later the General Convention (made up of laity) rejected the principle. Fifty-six bishops issued a statement expressing distress at the Convention's action.

Finally, on July 29, 1974, two retired and one resigned bishop, in the presence of a diocesan bishop who did not actually participate, proceeded to force the issue by "irregularly" ordaining eleven women deacons to the Episcopal priesthood in Philadelphia. After many debates on how the church should respond to the ministries of these women priests, in September 1976, the General Convention recognized the irregular ordinations and approved the ordination of women to the priesthood effective January 1, 1977.

Women's ordination in Presbyterianism is complicated by the fact that the Presbyterian/Reformed tradition engages in two types of ordination. Clergy are "set apart" by prayer and laying on of hands to a "ministry of Word and sacrament," *and* some lay leaders are "ordained" to a ministry of governance as "ruling elders."

In the 1880s and 1890s some presbyteries in the small frontier Cumberland Presbyterian Church began electing and ordaining women as "ruling elders," and in 1889, one of its presbyteries ordained a woman to a ministry of Word and sacrament. In the 1920s the Presbyterian Church in the U.S.A. (northern) voted to ordain women as ruling elders, but not as clergy. From 1930 to 1955, several efforts were made to give women full ministerial rights, but it was not until 1955 that the northern Presbyterians finally approved the ordination of women to the full ministry of Word and sacrament.

The more conservative Presbyterian Church in the U.S. (southern) defeated an overture to approve women as "ruling elders" in 1955. Finally in 1964, southern Presbyterians approved the ordination of women as deacons, ruling elders and ministers all at once. No one imagined, however, that many women would want, or would be qualified, to serve as pastors. In 1988, southern Presbyterians were reunited with several groups of northern Presbyterians to form the Presbyterian Church (U.S.A.).

The movement of women into ordained ministry in American Protestantism (including Presbyterian and Episcopal churches) in significant numbers dates from the early 1970s. Building upon the civil rights and women's liberation movements of the 1960s, seminary enrollments of women preparing for ordination in mainline Protestant denominations went from 4.7 percent in 1972 to 25.4 percent in 1992.[1] In 1977, Constant Jacquet collected data on women clergy in Protestant denominations for the National Council of Churches. At that time there were ninety-four ordained women in the Episcopal Church and 370 ordained women in the two Presbyterian denominations that have since merged to form the Presbyterian Church (U.S.A.).[2] Ten years later Jacquet reported that there were 796 women clergy in the Episcopal Church and 1,519 women clergy in the comparable Presbyterian bodies.[3] Data recently collected in a study by Hartford Seminary shows that in 1994 there were over 1,200 women clergy in the Episcopal Church and almost 2,400 women clergy in the Presbyterian Church (U.S.A.). These are dramatic increases. The 1990 United States Census reports that there are a little over a half million self-defined clergymen and -women in the population, and of those, 59,916 (nearly 11 percent) are women. This percentage is low because it includes all faith traditions, some of which (like the Roman Catholic Church) have no ordained women at all.

Sally Purvis has written a book that seizes "a moment in an era of tremendous social change." She has accepted the historical and statistical evidence around the movement of women into ordained leadership in American Protestantism and asked some important questions. How are women pastors "chipping away at the barnacles of gender stereotypes . . . as they go about their central vocation of priest and pastor to their people?" How does the experience of two effective female pastors relate to the essentialist arguments that there is a "woman's way of leadership?"

Purvis builds upon current "congregational studies" methodology, but tempers any "sympathetic reading" of the congregations she examines with a feminist analysis, "withholding sympathy from any structures, practices, and concepts that oppress women." Although she recognizes the importance of gender in her work, she concludes that "gender" is a fluid variable that cannot be pinned down. She writes that "gender turned out to signify constellations of fluctuating expectations rather than records of women's experience . . . ."

The book moves back and forth between narrative and analysis, describing developments in two strong congregations led by extremely competent women pastors, and reflecting on issues surrounding the power and authority of clergywomen in successful mainline congregations in a major southern city. Purvis's findings will be a resource for those engaged in issues of feminist theory and ethics, students of congregational research, and leaders responsible for theological education.

The most intriguing insight in the book comes when Purvis examines a lighthearted phrase offered by a parishioner in one of the congregations—"the best man for the job is a woman." Purvis shows that the ministries of the women pastors in these two congregations are part of a quiet revolution. In one sense these women participate comfortably in many of the existing leadership patterns formed and exercised by their male predecessors and by the historic assumptions surrounding male clergy. They are comfortable with power and authority. They are quite conventional. Yet at the same time, they are also women. They are content with their lives as heterosexual females, and they enjoy being womanly women. One of them is married, and one of them is single.

Purvis points out that contemporary feminist theory often focuses upon "difference" at the edges, or on the margins of what is normative, as the perspective necessary to destabilize the "hegemony of white male privilege." Marginality is used by oppressed groups to provide a new center from which to challenge the status quo. With these two women clergy, however, there is a different pattern of "transgression"—but one that challenges just as effectively past patterns and assumptions. These women pastors do what people expect them to do as women *and* as pastors. They do not deny the conventional expectations people have of them as women, *and* they do not disrupt conventional wisdom about the power and authority of effective pastoral leadership. They live comfortably with both, even though a "feminine female is supposed to be incommensurate with, if not oppositional to, strong organizational and political leadership abilities." By embodying "roles our social scripts say cannot be played by one person and roles that involve socialization processes that may be contradictory," they actually profoundly challenge unexamined assumptions about both women and clergy. In short, they *are* the best "men" for the job and they *are* women.

Such an unpredictable mixture of gender-based roles carries with it a cost. The cost is partially borne by the congregations. Each congregation took risks by calling a woman as its leader. The real cost, however, Purvis believes, is paid by the women themselves, causing them to live with the continual "dissonance of their own personalities, training, gifts, choices." Sometimes the source of the dissonance is tied to gender, as persons expect them to be more nurturing than they are simply because they are women. Sometimes the source of dissonance is tied to their role as clergy when their vulnerablity is unexpected and rejected, and their effective leadership is seen as inappropriate for a woman. Purvis's description of the tension whereby these women live with roles that are "of themselves conventional but transgressive in their combination" is the most important learning in this study. She suggests that the combination of conventional roles in unconventional ways will eventually help to "regender" roles and widen social tolerance for diversity: "Our study suggests that it is not just those who are blatantly unconventional who challenge conventions; rather those who embody conventional roles in unconventional combinations contribute to the breakdown of traditional gender expectations and aid in the reinscription of the gendering of roles and persons."

As a female leader in a historically male role (a seminary president), I find myself thinking, "So what else is new?" Yet this study gives textured testimony to the lives of many women in these times. It is not uncommon for women pioneering in traditional male roles to find that their days and their identities are at one and the same time reassuringly conventional and disturbingly uprooted. When I and other women in this situation are honest, however, we admit that we like the combination. There is an energy and a satisfaction that flows from such dissonance, holding great promise.

Barbara Brown Zikmund
President, Hartford Seminary

---

1. *Association of Theological Schools Fact Book,* 1982–83, (Vandalia, Ohio: 1983), 12, and 1992–93 (Pittsburgh, Penn.: 1993), 43.

2. Constant H. Jacquet, Jr., "Women Ministers in 1977," a report of the Office of Research, Evaluation and Planning, National Council of Churches, 1978, 11–12.

3. Constant H. Jacquet, Jr., "Women Ministers in 1986 and 1977: A Ten-Year View," *Yearbook of American and Canadian Churches* (1989), 261–66.

Preface

A basic question shaped my interest in and commitment to the project that resulted in this book: Is the leadership of women clergy having an impact on the churches they lead, and if so, how? Put another way, Are clergywomen making a difference in our parishes, and if so, what difference do they make? That question in its many forms arose out of my own former experience of pastoral ministry, in my case part-time, and the experience of many other women who are engaged in ordained ministries of various kinds in Protestant churches in the United States. We thought we were making some sort of difference, but we were not sure, and in any case we had a difficult time articulating that difference beyond anecdotes from our churches about "the lady pastor."

The opportunity to do actual extended, intentional, focused research on women's ministry, specifically on two churches whose senior clergy were women, has gone some way toward answering that question for me, but not all the way by any means. Some forms of the question have been sharpened—you will see many of them in the pages that follow. Others have become more confused, and still others have dropped out altogether. In many, many ways, the verdict is still out.

I choose the judgment language with care. As a Christian feminist, I view churches' responses to the gender revolution, and their contributions to the articulation and practices of the changes among us, as some indicators of faithfulness. I am mostly encouraged, though frequently wearied, by the process of incorporating the full humanity of women, including the leadership of women, into our corporate Christian lives. In that regard, this project has been a wonderful gift, and I am very pleased to be able to share at least portions of it with others. In shorthand form, part of what this study teaches us is that women clergy have more to fear from their churches than their churches do from them, and there seems to be plenty of love to go around. The women clergy whom I know start out brave, or get that way.

Given the organic nature of this project in my own personal and professional experience as woman, clergy, and scholar, I have to draw an arbitrary line around the research project itself in order even to begin to acknowledge all the help and support and wisdom others have shared with me.

I want to begin by expressing my gratitude to the Lilly Endowment for its commitment to the study of religion and to its generosity in supporting it. The Endowment provided a grant that enabled my research and that of several other faculty with whom I worked at Candler, who investigated various aspects of congregational life. I and my female research team quickly dubbed our generous supporter "Miz Lilly," and we want her to know we are grateful to her, and we miss her.

Next, I want to express my deepest gratitude to the courage, generosity, and hospitality with which the pastors and the churches accepted us and our questions and our presence. And a special thank you goes to all who agreed to be interviewed. Even if your specific stories do not appear, they shaped our account in profound ways. My respect and affection for all concerned should be obvious in the following account. I offer a special remembrance for "John Bates," who died on Palm Sunday, 1995.

Maggie Kulyk and Merry Porter, the research assistants for this adventure in congregational observation, are present in many, many ways in the pages that follow. Their commitment, insight, honesty, humor, and sheer common sense made even the stressful moments bearable and most of the moments fun. We really did function as a team, and although the written product is mine, the process was shared. I am grateful for their friendship, as well as for their labors.

Thank you also to my former colleagues at Candler School of Theology with whom the grant was shared: Pam Couture, Chuck Foster, Tom Frank, Robert Franklin, Gail O'Day, and Don Saliers. I am grateful for our many fertile exchanges. Thanks also to Nancy Ammerman, Jim Fowler, and Ted Hackett from the Candler faculty for their helpful consultations.

Outside consultants for this project were Letty M. Russell from Yale Divinity School and Beverly Wildung Harrison from Union Theological Seminary. Their work and their lives have gone a long way toward making a project like this possible. Their on-site observations and analysis of this specific study were immensely helpful for us and for the pastors with whom we were working. We are all indebted to their learning and wisdom.

Thanks is due to Westminster John Knox Press for the encouragement with which this project was met. Special thanks to Cynthia Thompson, who began the shepherding of a publishable product, and to Jon Berquist, who brought it home. I feel very fortunate to work with such knowledgeable and gracious people.

Many, many other persons responded with interest and helpful suggestions to this study during the four years it was under way, and I cannot include here all the acknowledgments that would be appropriate. Let me simply offer a general thank you.

Finally, a heartfelt thank you to my "GROUP," Judy, Margot, and Susan. I am, as always, grateful for and dependent on their love and support, including the prodding and teasing, in my own rather tumultuous process of change. And to Judy Wells, to whom this book is dedicated.

1   The Research Project

Ours is an era aware of its own deeply transitional nature. Change seems to outpace stability both conceptually and institutionally throughout the many dimensions of our individual and corporate lives. Old forms are breaking apart; new ones are not yet firmly in place. Or from another angle, old and new jostle each other in sometimes hostile and ever-shifting constellations of mores, values, and relationships.

In 1985, the Reverend Cameron Clark[1] became the first female rector in the Episcopal diocese of Atlanta. In 1991, the Reverend Suzanne Jefferson was installed as senior pastor in one of the largest Presbyterian churches in Atlanta; her church is the largest in her denomination headed by a woman. This is an account of their leadership and the lives of the churches that called them.

This study of two churches led by female pastors is centrally, though not exclusively, a portrait of change. Human lives are profoundly gendered, and seismic shifts have taken place and continue to take place in the gendering of roles, actions, attitudes, and understandings of gender itself.[2] These two pastors and their churches are both agents for and products of those changes. The powerful and effective leadership that the women provide to their congregations reflects a tripartite lens for viewing this process of gender revision: (1) their roles and their lives are products of changes that have already taken place and that allow them the opportunity to do what they do; (2) their lives and their work continue to clear away residues of resentment and reservations about women's ability to be effective pastoral leaders, and by extension, to assume other social and political leadership roles; (3) they and their churches are in the process of undergoing and negotiating social and theological change that has not yet emerged but that can be intuited and partially articulated.

Our study will document this complex process of change both

in the lives of the churches and in the lives of the pastors that lead them. The two pastors are outstanding in that few women yet have attained the level of authority and success they have; they are immensely talented persons. They are firsts, and they are exemplars in many ways. As such, they extend and widen the rethinking of gender at the cost of absorbing resistance and resentment regarding their trailblazing juxtaposition of gender and roles, and we will document that process. We can hope that the costs they bear based upon their place in the process of transition, and due to the stubborn residues of gendered expectations, will shift the balance toward more trust and broader scope for the performance of both genders. In their lives and work these female pastors are chipping away at the barnacles of gender stereotypes that block access to the whole range of social roles available to persons as they go about their central vocations of priest and pastor to their people.

Change is always a complex and dynamic process, shifting and slippery; documenting change is a bit like trying to photograph a moving train. In this case, we are not trying to capture just the train but also the surrounding landscape. The change that we study is located in the lives of the pastors, in the lives of their churches, and most important, in their shared lives as they interact with each other and with the social settings in which they participate. Thus this discussion will encompass change in three dimensions: in the lives and work of the pastors, in the churches they serve, and in the ways those interactions affect and are affected by the social narratives and dynamics of the congregations.

It may already be clear from these few words that our study of two churches in Atlanta led by female pastors did not support those findings that suggest that there is a "woman's way of leadership."[3] Gender proved to be more a category of expectations, and changing expectations in the case of our findings, than anything that could even loosely be called a "nature" or an "identity." Ours will be a counter-essentialist case study of the process of regendering even under conditions in which one might expect gender to be stable: mostly white, middle to upper-middle income, predominently heterosexual, conventional Protestant congregations.

The following is a document of change in a landscape of change. Women are enrolling in seminaries in record numbers even as the number of male applicants is down somewhat. The presence of female pastors in our churches, though now confined mostly to entry-level positions and/or churches in less desirable areas, will increase and deepen. If the two women in our research project can help us to predict what that increased presence will mean for the congregations they serve, then our findings suggest that the changes will be unpredictable based on any current expectations of gendered being or behaving. Rather the expectations themselves will undergo deep revision both in the lives of the congregations and in the lives of the women who lead them.

Questions about Power and Authority

Change on any level—personal, interpersonal, institutional, cultural—will involve shifts in the ways in which power and authority are exercised, or at least shifts in the personnel who exercise them. That is the thesis with which I began, and I believe it to be noncontroversial. We were trying to discern and define ways in which change did or did not take place in these churches as a result of their female leadership, so even in the most unfocused "getting-to-know-you" phase of this project, we were looking at various aspects of the lives of the congregations to identify understandings and practices of power and authority.

Some general definitions will be helpful. Power may be defined as "the ability to accomplish desired ends."[4] As such and in the abstract, then, power is an ethically neutral concept. Many feminists have distinguished between power that is "power over" and another power that is "empowerment"; in my volume *The Power of the Cross: Foundations for a Christian Feminist Ethic of Community*,[5] I use the terminology of "power as control" and "power as life and love." In the first case, desired ends are accomplished by using others as instruments of one's own purposes.[6] In the latter case, power is synergistic, springing from relationships of mutual respect and benevolence. Power as life and love is not experienced or understood to be a zero sum entity so that the more one person or group has, the less another must have. Rather, it images and exercises power as generative and boundless.

Authority can be defined as legitimated power. The instruments and processes of legitimation are as varied as the permutations of power, but however it comes about, authority is recognized as a source and wielder of power.[7]

The most abstract understandings of power and authority guided our initial research into the congregations, though the distinctions between the two kinds of power were always cognitively present in my observations. We found ourselves asking a number of questions: Whose will is effective? How does that efficacy get achieved? Who are the recognized authorities, both in terms of offices and in terms of congregational resources? How has the distribution and flow of power and authority changed/How are they changing because of the presence of these pastors? Or are they not changing at all? What, if anything, does the pastor's gender have to do with the nature and change in power and authority? Is there any discernible shift away from the power as control model and toward a more feminist conception and practice?

These were the complex questions that pulsed through our research from beginning to end and that will be both modified and partially answered in the chapters to follow.

Structuring the Research and Getting Started

After months of formulating research proposals, reading and talking about congregational research with colleagues, contacting research assistants, and developing budgets, it was time to begin the research. I had decided that I wanted to work in two churches both in order to limit the scope of the project and to obtain comparative data. I had also decided to eliminate as far as possible comparative complexities due to race, socioeconomic factors, and so on, and to do research in churches that represented what I came to call "my tribe," mostly white, of European origin, well-educated, mainline Protestant churches.

Since I had not been in Atlanta long and had done no church shopping myself, I began to ask people whether they knew of churches such as the ones I described that had a female senior pastor. Out of this very haphazard approach, two names kept coming up: Suzanne Jefferson and Cameron Clark. I called them to make appointments to discuss the project, to see if they would be interested in participating with their churches and/or to get their suggestions about other contacts. The responses were very different, theirs and mine.

Cameron and Bethany Episcopal Church

My first phone contact with Cameron was in January 1992, and she agreed to meet with me at the church that Saturday. I was struck on my arrival at how Episcopal the church looked, even without a "Norman tower" (a tall steeple). The stained-glass windows, the stone plaques, something of its aura fit with the sign in its yard. Cameron met me there, and what we later came to know as her style—direct, forthright, challenging, earthy, at times raucous—was very much in evidence during my first meeting with her. She took me to her colorful, comfortable, eclectically furnished office, listened to my description of the proposed project, and agreed that Bethany would be a good place for our research. She used the rest of our time together to ask me very direct questions about what she and the church would get out of it. The church is located near Emory University, and we were not the first people to want to study Bethany. It was clear to Cameron that she and Bethany would be a help to me, but what would I have to offer her and the church? What would they learn? What would be their risks?

Her directness startled me a bit, but I answered her questions as honestly and creatively as I could manage. By the end of our meeting, she had tentatively accepted the project and invited me to attend a Vestry meeting[8] to offer a formal proposal to the church. I left with a wild mix of feelings: relief that Cameron's questions had apparently been answered to her satisfaction, delight that I would have access to her and the church for the study, and some trepidation about working with her for the coming year. After our first meeting, I was both charmed and intimidated.

I attended the March Vestry meeting, and the Vestry was very receptive to the study. Their acceptance was clearly based in part on Cameron's endorsement, and I would not even have met with them had she not favored the project; but they also responded with genuine delight at the prospect of being the subjects of our re-search. The playfulness, openness, warmth, and humor of this con-gregation were well represented that night by its lay leaders.

Suzanne and St. Matthew's Presbyterian Church

Suzanne was a much more reluctant participant than Cameron, and her concern was due in large part to her much shorter tenure at St. Matthew's.[9] When I contacted her in January of 1992, she had been its pastor for only a few months, and she was still finding her footing. As this study will show, St. Matthew's can be tricky terri-tory to navigate.

I first contacted Suzanne by phone also in January 1992, and she was energetically flurried. She was in the middle of moving into the manse at St. Matthew's, she was overwhelmed by the newness and enormity of the job she'd taken on, and there was no possible way she could meet with me right then. I told her I could be free any time in the months ahead and said I'd call back in March when she thought she'd be able to talk to me. She was both intrigued and apprehensive about the project based upon the little I was able to tell her, but she was willing to meet to discuss it further after her life settled down a little bit.[10] We did meet in March, in her spa-cious, lovely, gracious, tasteful, even elegant office. St. Matthew's Presbyterian Church is a very large, beautiful brick church with a high, white steeple set on a "campus" of twenty-seven acres of mostly undeveloped land in northwest Atlanta. The church offices are upstairs, and after being greeted by the receptionist and waiting briefly, I was ushered into Suzanne's office by her secretary. Everyone with whom I spoke was gracious and friendly, and I was made to feel like a welcome guest in a well-run estate.

Our initial meeting was as open and honest as the telephone call had been. Suzanne was very revealing of herself and very protective of the church. She was deeply concerned about whether I would respect and honor what I had come to see, and she asked probing questions to be sure that "feminist" and "scholar" did not imply disdain for the church. My love for the Christian church and Christian congregations turned out to be the key ingredient in my initial relationship to St. Matthew's.

I met with the executive committee of the Session in May, and after some questions about what sorts of things I would be looking for and some concerns about confidentiality, they approved the project. Again, Suzanne's endorsement was crucial, and this time the acceptance was cordial and rather formal. The style of the executive committee was as representative of its church as the Vestry's had been. I then attended a Session meeting in September officially (and briefly) to inform them of the project and to introduce the research assistant who would be spending so much time with them. We were truly ready to begin.

The Research Begins

By the time I had finished the negotiations for approval of the project, I was fascinated by both churches and both ministers and the leadership of their very different congregations and felt no need or desire to look further. These settings offered everything I was looking for and more in terms of rich research possibilities.

I had hired two research assistants for the project, Merry Porter and Maggie Kulyk.[11] Both women had been students in classes I had taught, and the three of us correctly anticipated that we would enjoy working together. Given the nature of our research topic, power and authority in churches headed by women, and given the extensive and intensive nature of the research, it seemed to me prudent to let the two pastors and the two research assistants determine who would work in which church. The matches were made, and they were very good ones for all concerned.

For the first several months, from September 1992 until January 1993, our data-gathering process was as wide-ranging as possible. We purposely did not focus our research in such a way as to preclude any persons, activities, or transactions from our attention.

We simply observed, as openly and completely as we could, everything and everyone we could.

Out of this general attentiveness, patterns and conclusions began to form regarding the personalities of the churches and the operation of power and authority for both staffs and congregations. The feminist theologian Letty Russell visited from Yale Divinity School in February 1993 as an outside consultant to the project, and after her visit, which both confirmed our observations and sharpened our questions, we began to define focus issues that had arisen as potent examples of the play of power and authority in the churches. By the time our other outside consultant, feminist ethicist Beverly Harrison of Union Theological Seminary in New York City, visited us in May 1993, we were ready to begin to articulate our findings. Bev also confirmed our observations and helped us to refine our approach to presenting them.

Working, then, from our general sense about the nature of power and authority in the two churches, we identified a focus issue for each church. The focus issues are important not only because they give us one clear example through which to present our sometimes abstract claims about the operation of power and authority as we saw it, but even more so because they each reveal a deeper layer of that operation than some of our observations would have made possible. In each case, these events, or chain of events, enabled us to account for what had seemed to be anomalous behaviors, attitudes, and reactions but which became understandable and even predictable, given the deeper and more subtle rendering that the focus issues enabled.

Locating Us on the Congregational Studies Map

In his book *Places of Worship: Exploring Their History,* James P. Wind offers an excellent summary of the central assumptions and attitudes that shape contemporary congregational studies.[12] Rather than taking a set of criteria that a healthy church or a vital congregation ought to embody and measuring the adequacy of the group by those criteria, contemporary congregational studies assumes a stance rather like that of ethnography: it tries to get to know the congregation on its own terms, getting into its life, including its practices and symbols, to render an account of its lived reality.

Congregational studies in this mode are not so much interested in measuring churches as in meeting them and in getting to know them as they know themselves as much as possible. As in ethnography, the outsider's perspective offers a critical lens that may not be available from within, but the purpose of such study is not to critique but to describe and to offer evaluations based upon the values and *telos* of the church group itself.[13]

The contemporary students/scholars of congregational studies that I am citing were deeply influenced by the work of the late James Hopewell of Emory. Hopewell's methodological innovation centered on the use of "narrative" with his strategy of getting to know a congregation through the stories they told, and the stories they deliberately did not tell, and the story fragments that formed their lives together. Hopewell analyzed a church's life under the categories of "program, process, context, and identity,"[14] and he defined a church's identity as "the persistent set of beliefs, values, patterns, symbols, stories, and style that makes a congregation distinctive."[15]

One of the major contributions of Hopewell's approach was this focus on a church's identity. He claimed that getting to know a church meant paying attention to all of the elements that constitute its identity and to the way they interrelate in a church's life. Following Robert Redfield, he wrote of the "great tradition" and the "little traditions" which helped to define their self-understanding.[16] The great tradition is the classic tradition that constitutes the church's orthodox beliefs and practices. The little tradition by contrast is the way that orthodoxy is and is not lived out on the local level and the histories and beliefs and practices that constitute its particular embodiment of the great tradition.

Within the general approach just described, the "participant/observer" goes into a church to look at the variety of dimensions of congregational life and to note insofar as possible the way these dimensions manifest themselves in the lived texture of a church. Using my own terminology, the operative assumption is that every church has its own personality, and that getting to know a church is a process analogous to getting to know a person with her or his concentric circles of histories and traditions, range of experiences, high and low points, and partly formed and partly unformed future.

This sociological/ethnographic approach characterized our methodology to a large extent, especially during the first few months of our field research. We entered the project with genuine questions to answer, not specific theses to prove or disprove. We were open to finding out what was there in each of the two churches to the extent we could.

There are, however, two important qualifications to this approach that our research embodied. First, insofar as the participant/observer model is based upon ethnographic research, and to the extent that the ethnographer is a stranger from another tribe, the model does not fit us. I was aware of being engaged in the practice of studying my own tribe, with all of the advantages and pitfalls that it entails. My research assistants and I were strangers in the sense that we had been formed in and were members of other Christian denominations, and these specific churches with their ministers and members were new to us. However, socially, educationally, economically, racially, and even theologically, we were more like than unlike the folks we studied. We blended in very well, indeed, which also had its advantages as well as its disadvantages.[17] We could stand apart from, but not very far apart from, the persons we were observing. On the other hand, we could move quite close. Our own social, racial, economic, and theological realities enabled our intuitive as well as our cognitive connections with these churches.

I will describe in some detail in the next section several base points of the feminist convictions that shaped our analytical approach to the research. For now let me note the important feminist insight that all knowledge is perspectival.[18] There is no vantage point from which to view all aspects of human experience. Put another way, there is no neutral observation point, no "view from nowhere,"[19] which does not entail a particular perspective that includes some data and screens out other data. Thus groups that claim universality and accounts that purport to be objective are simply masking their perspective, usually by means of and in service of some degree of cultural hegemony or at least supremacy.

One way that we WASPs exhibit our cultural, social, and economic privilege is by remaining unaware of the peculiarities of our beliefs and our behavior. Rather we take as normal our sensibilities and practices. We do not, in other words, think of ourselves as ethnic. Ethnicity is that which belongs to those who are not WASP. A feminist approach provides a sensitivity to the particularity of any group, even a group who identifies itself as normative. In this case it provided us with lenses through which to view our own ethnicity with its mannerisms and customs and costumes, including its beliefs and practices about gender.

The second way in which our congregational research project departed from the standard accounts of contemporary congregational research as I have characterized them is that we used a specifically feminist approach. I will describe in more detail what I mean by that in the next section. For now, just let me say that our questions and interpretations were shaped by a feminist perspective. We were clear from the outset of the research that our perspective was foreign to the predominant discourses and formative narratives of the churches we were studying, and we were not tempted to impose our categories on them, their self-interpretations, or their stories. On the other hand, after the initial getting-to-know-you phase of our research was more or less complete, we used feminist analysis to focus our questions and to interpret our findings.

There is, of course, always a potential conflict between the "sympathetic reading" of a congregation recommended by Wind[20] and a feminist analysis of congregational life since a feminist approach is committed to withholding sympathy from any structures, practices, and concepts that oppress women. We can tell the patriarchal tale as we hear it, but we cannot present it through other than a critical lens. Thus feminist methodology modifies, and in some cases transgresses, the approach recommended in contemporary congregational studies.

This congregational research project, then, exists on the edge of contemporary congregational scholarship as it both depends on and departs from its assumptions and research methods.

Feminist Congregational Research

Mutual suspicion between feminists and mainstream Christian congregations is a common stance.[21] Collaborative research between the two is an uncommon activity. Taking that suspicion for granted, and in order to facilitate our research, we chose in some cases to accede to stereotypes of feminism that we encountered rather than to try to correct them. For example, we dropped the word feminist from our project presentations rather than try to convince the congregants that feminists were not necessarily hostile to Christian churches, and we bracketed the question of the pastors' feminist credentials as we engaged in our research.[22] In other words, we let the congregational suspicion be what it was and went about our work of gathering data without making an issue of the analytical lens through which we viewed it. On the other hand, the churches were told that I taught feminist courses at the seminary, we were never intentionally deceptive regarding our approach, and this volume will be thoroughly reviewed by each church before publication.[23] We were not secretive, and we were not confrontive. We simply let feminism mean whatever it meant to any group or individual.

The term feminist, then, can cover a wide range of meanings, even among those who call themselves feminist, and it is important to articulate the feminist commitments and convictions that fundamentally shaped this research project:[24]

1. Anthropological/theological convictions: Fundamental is the conviction that women are fully human. That is a deceptively simple claim. The history of Western culture and much of contemporary life in our society encompass beliefs and practices that are incompatible with that claim and make it difficult and at times impossible to live it out. The claim that women are fully human pushes beyond the possibility that women could be functional men and demands that women not have to be like men to be fully human. That is not an essentialist stance but rather an assertion about the viability and even desirability of differences in anthropological understandings, however the differences may arise. Furthermore, given Christian convictions, the full humanity of women is a God-given reality, and its denial transgresses not only against women but also against God.

2. Political strategies: Feminism comes with the commitment to help to reshape the world so that the full humanity of women can be embodied more and more fully. Such politics could be characterized as teleological pragmatism: whatever is necessary to move closer to the goal is what is required at the moment. That can mean that interim strategies may be appropriate and necessary even though they do not mirror the desired goal; a period of separatism may be such a strategy if women simply cannot experience the fullness of their being in the presence of men in certain settings. Furthermore, the test for teleological pragmatism is an ethical one and involves reflecting on the effects of one's behaviors and strategies on the least advantaged, a group that in our society usually consists of women and children of color. This political feminism is based upon a theoretical stance that the world is largely socially constructed, and that the constructions that constitute our common worlds systemically benefit some and disadvantage others. In order to make life better for the disadvantaged, we need to change those constructions, those structures of institutions and beliefs and practices.[25] Like the anthropological/theological convictions, this political feminism moves beyond liberalism and toward a radical revisioning of the possibilities and communal constructions of our lives together.

3. Feminist theory—or theories: Twenty years ago, in the beginning of this wave of feminism in our culture, feminists were disdainful of theorizing since the theory we had been trained to use was malestream. The early feminist writers focused on narratives of women's experience and especially on those places where women's experience escaped the theoretical/analytical categories of the classic theories. Some of the early insights included the identification and rejection of dualistic thinking, the privileging of female-female relationships of all kinds, the deeply gendered nature of our culture, and the articulation of a women's way of knowing and thinking, etc.[26]

With the growth of women's studies as a serious and legitimate academic and scholarly field, feminist theorizing is beginning to develop rapidly as an enterprise and as a body of literature.[27] North American feminists are beginning to engage feminists of other cultures.[28] African Americans are articulating womanist theory in which they identify the commonalities and differences with white North American feminists. [29] Conversations with French feminists are numerous. The work of Michel Foucault is discussed, appropriated, and criticized as is the work of earlier male theorists such as Freud and Marx.[30] Feminist theories function as the interpretive framework in which our analysis proceeds and our conclusions are drawn, including the refusal of feminist theories to claim univocal universal truth.

4. Feminist sensibility: This may be the most important factor of all in feminist analysis, and it may be the most difficult to articulate. It is the product of what is commonly called consciousness raising, and it involves an awareness, sometimes on a prelinguistic level, of the ways in which the world around us does not instantiate the claim that women are fully human but instead diminishes, trivializes, and exploits (or worse) female persons. An example will be more helpful than an elaborate description. Consider the following paragraph from a book by Celia Allison Hahn of the Alban Institute titled, *Sexual Paradox: Creative Tensions in Our Lives and in Our Congregations:*

> I want to speak here both to women and men, both to those who are feminist and those who haven't yet listened to them. I want to affirm the experience of men who, though they may not have greeted the present changes with enthusiasm, admit that justice demands some changes. I want to tell men that there is some promise for them in all these puzzling and distressing shifts, and point to some new ways of getting on with the practical challenges of working and living with women. And I want to suggest some alternative sources of energy to those who seek new vitality for mainline churches.[31]

She begins with a claim that she is speaking to both women and men. But notice the rest of the text. In this account that presumably addresses both women and men, she spends the rest of the paragraph addressing, assuring, and caring for men. In a world in which the needs of men almost always take precedence over the needs of women, in subtle and not-so-subtle ways, it is easy to overlook the fact that this account, and the book as a whole, is anything but balanced. A feminist sensibility enables us to notice, to record, and hopefully to transform the imbalance. Likewise, our feminist sensibilities enabled us to notice and to record such imbalances in the churches and in the lives of their ministers—some just as subtle, some much more blatant.

To summarize, feminism shaped the research and shapes this account of it in all these ways and through all these dimensions. We did not wear our feminism like a badge, and certainly not like a weapon, but it was always operative. It forms the experiential and theoretical contours of this project. I hope that some of the mutual suspicion between mainline Christian denominations and feminists can be dispelled a bit by its results.

The Fluidity of Gender[32]

As we began to try to correlate our emerging findings about understandings and practices of authority in the churches we studied with the gender of the pastors and the laity, we became increasingly aware of what a slippery category gender is. African American womanist literature has argued and analyzed the difficulty of speaking on behalf of women without regard for the other biological, social, and economic factors that constitute "women's experience."[33] We found this critical perspective to be important in our study of white, largely economically advantaged women as well. Qualities identified with woman sometimes turned out to be stereotypical characteristics that were not in fact representative of the lives of the women we observed. In other words, gender turned out to signify constellations of fluctuating expectations rather than records of women's experience, and the fluctuations themselves came to command our attention. We did, of course, record and take seriously the stereotypical understandings operative in the churches themselves. At times the stereotypes had a great deal of power, especially in St. Matthew's Presbyterian Church. However, in both churches the stereotypes functioned primarily as a standard against which women measured their lives rather than as an accurate articulation of their experience. It was clear even from the contrasts of these two churches that the kind and extent of power that congregants wielded outside the church in the community at large was very important to how gender served to empower or disempower persons in the churches. That is, the demographic profile of Bethany Episcopal Church shows a large percentage of people, male and female, trained for and employed in the helping professions in Atlanta; the congregation is replete with therapists and professors. St. Matthew's membership, on the other hand, includes many lawyers and prominent, influential business people, and in both categories almost all of the persons are male. As we might expect even from this small amount of information, gender roles are perceived and experienced more stereotypically at St. Matthew's than at Bethany. So in some sense, which I will define more carefully below, gender is socially constructed differently in the two congregations.

In addition, our observations taught us that regional considerations figured prominently in persons' ability to lead one of these congregations in particular, even though the pastors were female. In both cases, the churches' southern identity is an important feature of their congregational lives, and it is one factor, though only one factor, in their gender expectations.

One final introductory observation with regard to the fluidity of gender: in both cases, denominational identity is a much more important factor than gender in the power and authority of the women clergy. As Beverly Harrison commented when she consulted with our research team, both Suzanne and Cameron are "exemplars of their denominational formation."[34] They fit exactly the ministerial profile for their churches; they are the quintessential good minister and good priest according to their denominational standards. And their formation was largely malestream, though some feminist classes and issues were introduced. The formation process was not altered because they were women; nor had their theological education in the seventies been affected in any significant way by women's experience and insights as those might differ from men's. Thus their gender is officially a side issue, not relevant in any direct way to their effectiveness. We will see the way in which this formation—and these buried assumptions about the relevance or irrelevance of gender—are shared by their churches and are lived out by and take their toll on these two women. We will also note the dissonance that these buried assumptions create. We will, in other words, show some concrete ways in which gender is socially constructed, how the constructions differ depending upon the presence and weight of the other social factors that are present, and how these women and their churches are engaged in the process of reconstructing gender.

Weaving the Threads

As this brief introduction to some of the conceptual complexities of studying power and authority in churches led by women would indicate, there is no ready-made, coherent, whole picture that this account will simply record. I am describing and interpreting a large number of factors and lots of data from my own very specific perspective: white, upper-middle class, feminist Christian minister and scholar.[35]

In order to present this account in ways that do justice both to my perspective and interpretation, and to the possibility of other interpretations, I will offer a kind of dialogical account that moves from analysis to narrative and back again. I want to include enough of the stories so that women clergy, male clergy, students, laity in other churches, and denominational leaders can locate similarities and differences with persons and congregations here and can connect with and employ this account as best suits their needs. I also want to provide enough interpretation of what we observed so that those who are engaged in the issues of feminist theology and ethics, congregational research, and theological education can use our findings as a resource for their own work. Furthermore, the narrative will make the analysis more concrete and compelling, and the analysis will make the narrative more meaningful and coherent. To omit either one would be to truncate the usefulness of both.

It is time, now, to move into the stories.

NOTES

1. The names of all participants, and their churches, have been changed to protect some degree of anonymity. However, we are all clear that the situation of the churches and their pastors is sufficiently unusual so that anyone who knows Atlanta churches well, or a person from these denominations, is likely to know the real identities of the pastors and churches, if not particular congregants. Such is the current state of female leadership in our large Protestant churches.

2. The literature is now vast and any selection for citation is to some degree arbitrary. Simone de Beauvoir's *The Second Sex,* trans. H. M. Parshley (New York: Vintage Books, 1952), originally published in France in 1949, would, in my opinion, head any list. In addition, some general works that have been especially helpful for me are Vivian Gornick and Barbara K. Moran, eds., *Woman in Sexist Society: Studies in Power and Powerlessness* (New York: Basic Books, 1971); from the 1980s: Hunter College Women Studies Collective, *Women's Realities, Women's Choices* (New York: Oxford University Press, 1983); Susan Brownmiller, *Femininity* (New York: Simon and Schuster, 1984); Audre Lorde, *Sister/Outsider* (Trumansburg, N.Y.: The Crossing Press, 1984); bell hooks's works, including *Feminist Theory: From Margin to Center* (Boston:

South End Press, 1984), *Talking Back: Thinking Feminist/Thinking Black* (Boston: South End Press, 1989), and *Yearning: Race, Gender and Cultural Politics* (Boston: South End Press, 1990). Also, Nancy Fraser, *Unruly Practices: Power, Discourse and Gender in Contemporary Social Theory* (Minneapolis: University of Minnesota Press, 1989); Iris Marion Young, *Throwing Like a Girl and Other Essays in Feminist Philosophy and Social Theory* (Bloomington, Ind.: Indiana University Press, 1990); Donna J. Haraway, *Simians, Cyborgs and Women: The Reinvention of Nature* (New York: Routledge, 1991); Susan Bordo, *Unbearable Weight: Feminism, Western Culture and the Body* (Berkeley, Calif.: University of California Press, 1993); and Judith Butler's studies, *Gender Trouble: Feminism and the Subversion of Identity* (New York: Routledge, 1990) and *Bodies That Matter: On the Discursive Limits of "Sex"* (New York: Routledge, 1993). And there are many, many more.

3.   See the study by Sally Helgesen, *The Female Advantage: Women's Ways of Leadership* (New York: Doubleday, 1990). Her work is consonant with Carol Gilligan's immensely influential *In a Different Voice: Psychological Theory and Women's Development* (Cambridge, Mass.: Harvard University Press, 1982) and Mary Field Belenky, Blythe McVicker Clinchy, Nancy Rule Goldberger, Jill Mattuck Tarule, *Women's Ways of Knowing: The Development of Self, Voice and Mind* (New York: Basic Books, 1986). Our research is too limited in scope to provide a counter general thesis to these studies. Furthermore, the latter two works are important in analyzing some of the various ways gender functions in the socialization process in this culture. We learned from our study that some of the behavior and attitudes we had been led to expect regarding distinctive female leadership styles did not characterize the clergywomen we observed. Also see, by contrast to our study, Robin Tolmach Lakoff, *Talking Power: The Politics of Language in Our Lives* (New York: Basic Books, 1990). Lynn Rhodes's *Co-Creating: A Feminist Vision of Ministry* (Philadelphia: Westminster Press, 1987) was a study of women clergy who were intentional about trying to minister in accordance with feminist values and practices, and it provides a nice contrast to the more eclectic leadership styles in our study.

4.   Letty M. Russell, *Household of Freedom: Authority in Feminist Theology* (Philadelphia: Westminster Press, 1987), 21.

5.   Sally B. Purvis, *The Power of the Cross: Foundations for a Christian Feminist Ethic of Community* (Nashville: Abingdon Press, 1993). The two kinds of power often intertwine, of course, but I have argued that in ordinary experience they are commonly distinguishable.

6.   That process can take various forms, of course. Iris Marion Young very helpfully distinguishes between oppression and domination and lists the "five faces of oppression" as follows: exploitation,

marginalization, powerlessness, cultural imperialism, and violence. While one might take issue with some details of her analysis, especially her less than full account of the power of oppressed people, she helps to dispel any sense that oppression is simple or univocal. See Iris Marion Young, *Justice and the Politics of Difference* (Princeton, N.J.: Princeton University Press, 1990), esp. chapter 2.

7. Some suggestions for helpful discussions of issues of power and authority are Carter Heyward, *Touching Our Strength: The Erotic as Power and the Love of God* (San Francisco: Harper & Row, 1989); Elizabeth Janeway, *Powers of the Weak* (New York: Knopf, 1980); Letty M Russell, *Household of Freedom;* James Poling, *The Abuse of Power: A Theological Problem* (Nashville: Abingdon Press, 1991); Richard Sennett, *Authority* (New York: Knopf, 1980); Iris Marion Young, *Throwing Like a Girl.*

8. A Vestry is the governing board of lay leadership in an Episcopal church. As we will see, a Session is the comparable body in a Presbyterian church.

9. At the time of my initial contact with the two pastors, Cameron had been at Bethany for over six years, and Suzanne had been at St. Matthew's for less than one year.

10. After we hung up, I remembered some photographs that I had taken of a statue depicting a somewhat abstract female form. She is standing with legs widely spread and one hand on either side of her head, and there are a number of small abstract human figures hanging onto various parts of her body: a woman being drained and exhausted by demands all over her. I sent Suzanne a copy of the photograph with a note, and I got a lovely note in return. It was, and continues to be, very important to her to be heard and understood. Her ability to trust me, the research assistant, and this project was a function of our ability to hear and understand her. I've thought that the photograph was a good beginning.

11. These are their real names; anonymity is not appropriate in this case.

12. James P. Wind, *Places of Worship: Exploring Their History* (Nashville: American Association for State and Local History, 1990), 17–21. See also Jackson W. Carroll, Carl S. Dudley, and William McKinney, eds., *Handbook for Congregational Studies* (Nashville: Abingdon Press, 1989) and Carl S. Dudley, Jackson W. Carroll, and James P. Wind, eds., *Carriers of Faith: Lessons from Congregational Studies* (Louisville, Ky.: Westminster/John Knox Press, 1991) for further helpful discussions about contemporary congregational studies.

13. Tom Frank's excellent monograph *Vital Congregations—Faithful Disciples: Vision for the Church,* Foundational Document of the United Methodist Council of Bishops (Nashville: Graded Press, 1990) is a good example of a congregational study that asks

questions about vitality from the perspective of the congregations themselves.

14. Hopewell's work is described with clarity and simplicity in Carroll, Dudley, McKinney, *Handbook,* 13.

15. Ibid., 12.

16. Ibid., 26.

17. Other congregational researchers may also be more participant and less observer than they record. Our awareness of our place among them was formative for our research.

18. Donna Haraway's essay "Situated Knowledges" is the most compelling and comprehensive discussion I have found of feminist epistemology. *Simians, Cyborgs and Women: The Reinvention of Nature* (New York: Routledge, 1991).

19. Thomas Nagel, *The View from Nowhere* (New York: Oxford University Press, 1986). This is Thomas Nagel's discussion of subjectivity and objectivity in human knowing. While I do not agree with every aspect of his analysis, I do like the title.

20. James P. Wind, "Leading Congregations, Discovering Congregational Culture," *Christian Century,* (February 3–10, 1993): 105–114, 107.

21. See Letty Russell, *Church in the Round: Feminist Interpretation of the Church* (Louisville, Ky.: Westminster John Knox, 1993), esp. the preface, 11–15. There are exceptions, of course. See, for example, Anne Carr, *Transforming Grace: Christian Tradition and Women's Experience* (San Francisco: Harper & Row, 1988).

22. Though the feminist credentials, or lack thereof, of the ministers in this study were not determinative of the extent to which their female leadership changed or did not change their churches, it was interesting to note the ways in which the two women responded to the label. Suzanne initially rejected the label feminist; she said that feminists were angry with the church, and the church had been the most nurturing place she had experienced. By the end of the study, she embraced the label because she came to see it less as descriptive of a stance of anger toward the churches and more as a position of advocacy for the lives of all women. Cameron seems both more comfortable with the label and less concerned about it. Both before and during seminary she had participated in feminist studies, and her descriptions of some of her confrontations with the male clergy in her denomination and her stands on social issues indicate feminist leanings.

23. Part of our agreement with each church includes their option to review the entire manuscript before publication to ensure accuracy and privacy.

24. For an excellent article on the topic see Margaret Farley, "Feminist Ethics," in *The Westminster Dictionary of Christian Ethics,* ed. James F. Childress and John Macquarrie (Philadelphia: Westminster, 1986): 229. My summary is personal but is in substantive agreement with Farley's analysis.

25. My use of the phrase social construction does not mean that I am a structuralist. Rather, an astute reader will hear echoes of Foucault and deconstructionists and other postmodern thinkers. An especially astute example of the process of social construction not only of institutions but even of understandings of what we usually think of as givens can be found in Nancy Fraser's *Unruly Practices: Power, Discourse and Gender in Contemporary Social Theory* (Minneapolis: University of Minnesota Press, 1989) and especially in the chapter titled "Women, Welfare, and the Politics of Need Interpretation." See also the work of Judith Butler, especially her latest volume, *Bodies That Matter: On the Discursive Limits of "Sex"* (New York: Routledge, 1993).

26. See Gilligan, *Different Voice* and Belenky, *Women's Ways*. See also Carol P. Christ and Judith Plaskow, eds., *Womanspirit Rising: A Feminist Reader in Religion* (San Francisco: Harper & Row, 1979) and Rosemary Radford Ruether, *Sexism and God-Talk: Toward a Feminist Theology* (Boston: Beacon Press, 1983) for early discussions of some of the central themes in feminist theology.

27. A check of the Emory library holdings in the summer of 1993 showed eighty-five listings under "feminist theory." Of that eighty-five, the earliest were the three volumes that were published in 1989, five more were published in 1990, and the rest were produced in the last three years.

28. In the area of theology see Katie Geneva Cannon, Ada Maria Isasi-Diaz, Kwok Pui-lan, Letty M. Russell, eds., *Inheriting Our Mothers' Gardens: Feminist Theology in Third World Perspective* (Philadelphia: Westminster Press, 1988); Susan Thistlethwaite, *Sex, Race and God: Christian Feminism in Black and White* (New York: Crossroad, 1989); and Sharon D. Welch, *A Feminist Ethic of Risk* (Minneapolis: Fortress Press, 1990). The issue of appropriation of the work of the oppressed by the (relatively) advantaged remains a concern in interracial feminist/womanist dialogue in this culture. It is one that the above-cited works take seriously, if not always with perfect sensitivity.

29. Womanist theology/ethics includes Katie G. Cannon, *Black Womanist Ethics* (Atlanta: Scholars Press, 1988); Patricia Hill Collins, *Black Feminist Thought: Knowledge, Consciousness, and the Politics of Empowerment* (New York: Routledge, 1990); Emilie M. Townes, *Womanist Justice, Womanist Hope* (Atlanta: Scholars Press, 1993) and Emilie Townes, ed., *A Troubling in My Soul: Womanist Perspectives on Evil and Suffering* (Maryknoll, N.Y.: Orbis Books, 1993); Delores Williams, *Sisters in the Wilderness: The Challenge of Womanist God-Talk* (Maryknoll, N.Y.: Orbis Books, 1993). This is just a small sample of current literature from only one field.

30. A short sample includes Judith Butler and Joan W. Scott, eds., *Feminists Theorize the Political* (New York: Routledge, 1992); Irene Diamond and Lee Quinby, eds., *Feminism and Foucault: Reflections*

on Resistance (Boston: Northeastern University Press, 1988); Jana Sawicki, *Disciplining Foucault: Feminism, Power and the Body* (New York: Routledge, 1991); Chris Weedon, *Feminist Practice and Poststructuralist Theory* (London: Basil Blackwell, 1987).

31. Celia Allison Hahn, *Sexual Paradox: Creative Tensions in Our Lives and in Our Congregations* (New York: Pilgrim Press, 1991): viii.

32. Sally B. Purvis, "The Fluidity of Gender," lecture delivered to the Society of Christian Ethics, annual meeting, January 1994.

33. See the work of bell hooks cited in note 2 above and the womanist literature cited in note 23 above. For a fascinating discussion of race and gender outside the field of theology see Toni Morrison, ed., *Race-ing Justice, En-gendering Power: Essays on Anita Hill, Clarence Thomas, and the Construction of Social Reality* (New York: Pantheon Books, 1992).

34. Conversation with author and Maggie Kulyk, research assistant for St. Matthews, May 1993.

35. I was ordained a minister in the United Church of Christ in 1983 and served a church part-time for eight years.

2   The First Woman Rector

A Prism of Past and Present

There was even more activity than usual at Bethany Episcopal Church on the August morning in 1993: the Bishop of the diocese of Atlanta was present to receive Julia as Episcopal deacon.[1] Julia, the wife of a former rector, has been a beloved pastoral presence, friend, and mentor of members of Bethany Episcopal Church for two generations or more. She was a deaconess of the Anglican Church of Canada before she came with her husband to Atlanta in 1953 and had significant responsibility and authority in that position. However, as her husband told her, "one priest in the family is enough,"[2] and besides, women could not be ordained as priests. So she nurtured and served the church as a layperson even after her husband's death in 1975. Now, forty-nine years after her original orders, and "having passed physical, psychological, and theological examinations and having had her paperwork verified"[3] Julia was being "transformed from being a deaconess in the Anglican Church of Canada to being a deacon in the Episcopal Church." She was seventy-five years old.

It is important to remember throughout this account of two contemporary Christian congregations headed by women that the decision to ordain women, whenever it took place in different denominations, and the decision to call a woman as a senior clergyperson, whenever and wherever that decision was enacted, are part of a long history of women's leadership in Christian congregations and denominational groups of all sorts. Mary Sudman Donovan, a scholar of women's contributions to the Episcopal Church writes:

> My contention is that in the period between 1850 and 1920 women transformed the Episcopal Church by providing the labor force and the moral initiative to establish social-service ministries (schools, hospitals, orphanages, neighborhood centers, etc.), by

structuring the support system necessary to enable missionary expansion, and by developing a communications network that fostered a diocesan rather than a parochial identity for individual church members.[4]

Like the women in Donovan's study, Julia resisted confrontation with church authorities of all kinds, her husband included, and saw herself as a servant of the church, not an instrument of its change. She was, of course, both. Thus, Julia's story and Cameron's story overlap and intersect in some obvious and subtle ways. Cameron herself articulates the important role that Julia played and continues to play at Bethany and the extent to which the congregation's knowledge and trust of her leadership helped to mold their understandings of authority, power, and leadership in general. The first woman rector moved into a church in which women's leadership could be trusted. Julia's reception as deacon just at the time that our field research was ending provides an important reminder that there is both continuity and change with regard to women's official and unofficial roles in our churches.

Welcome to Bethany Episcopal Church

The worship service at Bethany that morning was much like it usually is. I entered the narthex[5] to the usual cheerful bustle and was greeted warmly by a couple of parishioners I recognized.[6] John was already at the organ at the back of the church playing the prelude, and the choir was in place.

Even on an ordinary Sunday, quiet, meditative prayer before the service is almost impossible. At the very least, it requires intense concentration to screen out the busy, cheerful, getting-settled process. People talk to one another, priests and acolytes gather in the back of the church to prepare for the procession, and the children, the ever-present, beloved children of Bethany create an air of contained chaos and liveliness that is such a part of that community.

If your image or your experience of an Episcopal service is that it is hushed, sedate, even stilted, then Bethany will be a surprise. The service is richly liturgical without being formal, reverent without being stiff. The space of the sanctuary is open, with vaulted wood ceilings and white walls, some stained-glass and some clear windows; it is full of light. The floor is not carpeted, and the acoustics were carefully designed not to swallow sound. So the rustlings, the movements, the page turnings, the whispered conversations and, of course, the children, provide a warm and informal family atmosphere for worship.

The reception provided a kind of icon for the changing nature of women's official options in the church that the service itself embodied. Gathered at the altar were the rector, the assistant rector, and the newly received deacon, all of whom were women. The bishop and the senior warden[7] were men. There was no special consciousness of gender during that hour that I could discern, although untold official and unofficial hours of careful attention to and work on behalf of women had to precede it. Now, having two women priests is the day-to-day reality of this congregation. On this occasion a wonderful, gifted, wise, spirit-filled woman was having her calling officially acknowledged, and the whole church was celebrating. The morning, then, was an icon of this church at least, in all its richness, liveliness, and playfulness, and mostly unself-conscious but deeply revolutionary life.

A Look into the Past[8]

Near the turn of the century, a group of people led by a woman initiated the establishment of Bethany Church in what was then the eastern part of Atlanta, an area now known as "Little Five Points." As the church historian wrote:

> In the beginning was a dream and this dream harbored the idea that a new church was needed badly in the Edgewood section of Atlanta. The Almighty planted this dream in the soul of Mrs. . . . , and together with her husband, they set about the slow but rewarding task of crystallizing the dream.[9]

After several years of "house church," Bethany began as a mission church of the diocese in 1898. The first Vestry organized in 1900 with a membership of five men. By 1908 the membership (and hence the budget) had grown sufficiently to become a full-fledged parish, and Bethany called the first rector in 1909.

Although the official leadership of Bethany was all male, females were active and influential in this church from the beginning. As noted above, a woman was the guiding force, and apparently the source of much of the energy, in the founding of Bethany. A women's group, nationally called the Auxiliary and locally named the Guild was the "development office" of the church and raised most of the money for the expansion of the building in the early 1900s and for various outreach programs in the immediate community and beyond.[10]

In 1922 the church buildings were bought by Gulf Oil Company, and for a while the congregation met in a local school. However, by the end of 1923 they had moved to a second location near the first. The expansion of the church, both human and financial, was curtailed by the Depression, but a special appeal by the rector was successful in avoiding a foreclosure by the bank, and the church remained in operation throughout that time. By the end of the 1930s it was growing again, and by the late 1940s it was a healthy, prosperous church.

Up to this point, the history is fairly typical of a developing, growing, and expanding church community with a string of male priests and the ongoing and powerful though unofficial support of the women of the church. In this context, there is an incident in the history of Bethany that is amusing to recall but that was, no doubt, traumatic to experience: in 1914, while it was in its first location, the church bought some property nearby in the hopes of moving and building a new church. In 1920, the property had to be sold for back taxes because the church and the diocese each thought the other was paying the taxes on the land, although, unfortunately, neither did. From my perspective two generations later, it seems that the business acumen of the female Guild might profitably have been employed in a more official capacity in the area of church finances!

By the late 1940s, the neighborhood that Bethany had called home was undergoing transition from a fairly stable residential neighborhood to a more transient place as large homes were converted into boarding houses and more businesses opened in the area. There was some talk about moving the church site closer to Emory University, and with the arrival of the Jacobses in 1953, the process began concretely to develop.

Part of the initial delay in moving Bethany's location was due to the difficulty the church experienced in finding a buyer for their old buildings. Another part of the problem was the scope of the new building that the congregation had in mind: It was to be just slightly smaller than a cathedral! Finally, however, the old church property did sell, and in the transition the activities of the church moved to various parts of Emory and into people's homes.

As I mentioned, the move to the Emory area transpired during the tenure of Julia Jacobs and her husband, Dr. Jacobs. He was rector of Bethany for eighteen years, from 1953 to 1971, and his eventual resignation was prompted by ill health.[11] Dr. Jacobs was convinced from the outset that Bethany's future depended upon moving to a location closer to Emory. We can surmise that the move would have personal appeal for Dr. Jacobs since he had two Ph.D.s and probably felt at home in a more academic environment. When land became available, and the church did not have the money on hand to purchase the $25,000 piece of property, Dr. Jacobs called a meeting of the Vestry. He and Julia pledged $1,000, asked each of them to do the same, and then found enough additional thousand-dollar pledges in the congregation to buy the land. The record suggests that this approach was typical of his leadership, and the general impression of the early years, at least, is of quiet growth and a fairly stable church life.

As the years went by, the church was completed. The fifties turned into the sixties and then into the late sixties, by which time Bethany acquired a reputation as a very conservative place, and the written record and some oral history suggest tension below the surface. The best illustration is the resignation of two senior wardens in 1967. The first resigned to join the Anglican Orthodox denomination. He said he loved Dr. Jacobs and Bethany, but he objected to the Episcopal Church hierarchy because it had joined the "godless ecumenical" groups, the National Council of Churches and the World Council of Churches, and he wanted to be in a church that "retains the worship service and traditions of the Anglican Church and the doctrine as set forth in *The Book of Common Prayer.* . . . "[12] Eight months later another senior warden resigned for reasons that are not so clear but that may have had to do with the approval of lay readers to administer the chalice during Holy Communion.

In the Bethany *News* the rector had this comment:

> One resigned because of church involvements in the "social revolution." The other resigned because "Bethany" was not involved enough. However, we hope to avoid extremism from either side. It is also possible that our senior wardens thought too much of that office. According to canon law a senior warden is not a presiding officer in charge of church operations. He, like the junior warden, works under the direction of the rector of the church.[13]

This is a fascinating little document, and it suggests that deep tensions were building around various aspects of the social change of the late 60s and early 70s, but were not allowed to be processed. Leaving aside considerations of personality quirks that seem always to be a part of the political process in any church congregation, the resignation of two senior wardens within eight months of each other would have been painful for the church as a whole. The rector's response was to say, in effect, "I'll respond to conflict here by asserting my authority. The senior wardens work for me." That was not, of course, an unusual attitude, or leadership style, for a priest of that time.

In a private conversation with a non-Bethany member, I learned that the political tensions in the church during these years ran deep indeed. The rector naively assumed that the church could be insulated from the politics of the world, an attitude suggested by his brief response cited above. In fact, at least some elements of the congregation at Bethany had become deeply conservative, even reactionary, and there were rumors that groups like the John Birch Society were holding meetings in the basement of the church without the rector's full awareness of their political stances or agendas. One can only surmise the power struggles that went on beneath the surface, never fully processed or even spoken, but against which the perhaps bewildered rector simply asserted his clerical authority.

The currents of change and resistance to change swirled even more rapidly and came to the surface in many ways in 1971 when a new rector, Don McGee, was appointed after Dr. Jacobs's resignation due to ill health.[14] Don's first and main task at Bethany was to introduce the liturgical changes that would be brought about by the new Episcopal *Book of Common Prayer*. The final form was widely adopted in 1976, but the church had instructed its priests to help prepare the people for the changes. There were a series of trial liturgies, and in accordance with their identification of the Eucharist as the primary rite for a Sunday, churches introduced more frequent communion services. Anyone who cannot remember that time, or anyone who was not part of a liturgical reformation, may find it difficult to understand the pain and anger of people who were being asked—no, told—to change the way they had worshiped all their lives. For many persons, the changes felt invasive, intrusive, and just plain wrong. The revision of the prayer book, and the revised practices that it involved, affected very precious, intimate areas of people's lives, and resentment was widespread.

Not only was the new rector imposing difficult liturgical changes, his personal and clerical style were dramatically different from what the congregation was used to after eighteen years of Dr. Jacobs. Don was much more informal, preferring to be addressed by his first name. Casual in manner and dress, he was "laid back" in the vernacular of that time. If the John Birch Society ever really had met in the basement of Bethany, it was clear that they were no longer welcome, and the laity began to be invited to participate in the life of the church in some new ways.

One aspect of those changes was the introduction of women to the Vestry of the church. While the women's groups had been active since the beginning of the congregation, and their support of the church in terms of activities and finances continued to be essential for the church's survival, they were not in positions of official authority in the ruling body of the church. That changed with the times and the revised national canons, and the changes were implemented under Don's leadership. The first woman was nominated to the Vestry in 1973, and she was made the senior warden the next year. Two years later, Bethany had its first woman intern in process for Holy Orders. From the mid-1970s on, women and men have worked together without rigid gender roles, a point I will return to below.

Along with liturgical and structural changes at Bethany, Don brought an emphasis on social action ministry for the whole church that emphasized the plight of street people and the poor in general. Bethany had always been involved in mission work, primarily through the agency of the women in the church as I described above, but there does not seem to have been a strong emphasis on what we might now call solidarity between the members of Bethany and those less fortunate in the wider society. That sense of solidarity seems to have been a mark of Don's ministry and something that he brought into Bethany that engendered various degrees of discomfort among the congregation. As one current member observed, every minister has one sermon. His was, "We are all broken, and through Christ we are made whole."[15] We do not have her characterization of Dr. Jacobs's one sermon, since she joined after he left, but it is clear that McGee was a dramatic departure from his predecessor and in the position of making broad and deep changes that met with various degrees of resistance and acceptance.

Furthermore, Don has been described as laid back, but shy. He was awkward in group social gatherings, and while he was warm to the people who sought him out and was a loving and effective pastor one on one, he was not perceived as someone who reached out to the congregation.

After what appear to have been eight very difficult years at Bethany due largely to the immensity of the current changes inside and outside the church, Don moved on to diocesan work. An interim priest from Emory was assigned for a short time, and the church called its next rector in 1980. The next rector's time at Bethany was dominated by his personal crisis—a very painful abandonment by his wife and a subsequent divorce. Understandably, the personal situation deeply compromised his ability to provide forceful, clear leadership for the church. There was apparently a lot of affection between this rector and many persons at Bethany, but the personal issues eclipsed professional effectiveness. The Bishop of Atlanta's regulations required that the rector resign from the parish when he decided to remarry, and the resolution of his personal pain marked the end of his relationship to Bethany.[16]

The task of the search committee at this point was to find someone who could lead the church. It wanted a priest with energy, vision, and the ability to motivate others, and someone who seemed relatively stable and happy. It had not planned on calling a woman, though it was open to the possibility from the beginning, and it did not hesitate to do so when she proved to be the embodiment of all of the qualities the church so badly needed. In the spring of 1985, Cameron Clark was called to be the ninth rector of Bethany Episcopal Church.[17] Here is how it happened.

The Search Process

North American society, the Christian churches, the Episcopal denomination, and Bethany Episcopal Church had undergone dizzying changes in the preceding thirty years. By and large, Bethany had experienced those changes without a strong sense of leadership from its rectors, and leadership was above all what they wanted as they began their search in 1984.[18] More precisely, the church was looking for someone who could be both a manager and a pastor, caring and dependable. There is consensus that Don McGee accomplished what he was sent to Bethany to do: he was to lead the congregation through the liturgical changes demanded by the new prayerbook, which were anything but trivial, and to "cleanse the Temple" of some reactionary elements that had gotten lodged in the corners, if not the heart, of the church.[19] The next rector was also well liked, but his personal pain had required that the congregation minister to him, which, it is important to note, they did with compassion, affection, and patience. Several well-liked priests filled in during the search process, but now it was time to find a rector who would be a dynamic, efficient leader.

The Episcopal diocese of Atlanta offered consultation, and the search process was conducted very carefully and by the book. A parish profile was drawn up, and the needs and character of the church were well articulated. The search committee decided early on that any offer it made would be based on consensus—that in such an important matter, simple majority would not be enough.

Out of the leadership vacuum created by recent events at Bethany, a strong group of lay leaders had emerged, and from that group, a search committee was formed. Not all were long-time members of Bethany, but all were dedicated to the church.

From the beginning, people on the search committee opened the process to female applicants. The committee was "flooded with applications" from persons of both genders[20] because the job was so appealing, and the committee was clear that they would seriously consider all persons regardless of gender. They were not naive, however, about the potential difficulties the congregation might have accepting a female rector. The committee let it be known from the outset that a female rector was a possibility, and it reached out to the congregation in various ways for feedback and discussion about a number of issues, including gender. From the beginning, the committee's concern was to find the best person for the job, and they were not prejudging a requirement about gender in making that decision.[21]

After several months of hard work, the committee made a decision and called a male priest from another southern state. He turned down the offer.

The committee regrouped and basically started over. Its members continued to read profiles and to interview people. The final decision came down to a choice between a male and a female, and the vote was by secret ballot. Committee members believed that both of the final candidates would make good rectors and that they could live with whatever decision was made. However, the vote, though not unanimous, was not even close. In fact, the committee had agreed from the beginning that no vote would be taken unless the candidates were agreeable to all the members of the committee and unless every committee member would be willing to join in a unanimous recommendation to the Vestry. That is what happened.

On Easter Sunday, 1985, the senior warden announced to the congregation that the Reverend Cameron Clark accepted the Vestry's call to become rector of Bethany Episcopal Church, and the first female rector in the diocese of Atlanta. There was a report by the senior warden in the church newsletter, and the final paragraph reads as follows:

> Much will be made of the precedent set by this call. It was not our goal to set a precedent, however; our goal was to call the priest that God wanted us to call. I am convinced that we have done that, and I look forward with great joy and excitement to our ministry together with [Cameron Clark].[22]

Issues of Power and Authority

In a recent interview, Julia Jacobs spoke of some regrets that she had not studied for the priesthood.[23] As I noted at the beginning of this chapter, some of the reasons she did not were personal; her husband was very clear that one priest in the family was enough, and, of course, it was he. She also wanted to stay home with her children, and in spite of being told she could not bear children, they had three. However, the major block in her path to the priesthood was not a function of her own choice: women were not ordained into the priesthood in the United States until 1974 and not regularly and canonically until 1977. Julia had been ordained a deaconness of the Anglican Church in Canada, but when she came with her husband to the United States, she did not seek to have her orders recognized in this country. Julia functioned, as many priests' and ministers' wives functioned, as unofficial pastors to the congregation to which their husbands had been called. She was trusted, admired, and respected. She provided extensive pastoral care for that congregation, care that the church might not have gotten from her more formal husband. She organized groups of women, but she refused to do so much that other women might not take responsibility for the women's activities. In the terms of this study, she clearly had power, but she did not have institutional authority. She was an effective leader because of personal qualities and skills, not because she was the bearer of an institutional role.

Cameron Clark, on the other hand, had and embraced the opportunity to combine an array of personal capabilities with the professional formation and institutional certification that she would need to function as a full professional in the priesthood of the Episcopal Church. She was no more dependent on the institution than was Julia to create her abilities to lead and to pastor. She was, however, in a position to take advantage of institutional changes that enabled her to become a priest and thus take her place as an official leader of the church.

Cameron came to Bethany in 1985 as one of the first generation of female priests in the Episcopal Church. She was in seminary when the first women were regularly ordained by the Episcopal Church; Cameron herself was ordained a deacon in 1978 and a priest in 1979.

As we survey the history of Bethany and listen to people as they recall Cameron's arrival there, the image that comes to mind is of a whirlwind bursting through the doors of the church. After six years as a parish assistant and day school chaplain at a church north of Atlanta, Cameron was ready to take on the challenges of being a rector, and she did so with an energy level that still leaves people breathless in the retelling of it. The search committee that recommended Cameron was clear that it wanted a strong leader, and there was already in place a cadre of powerful lay leaders who had more or less run the church for several years. However, the energy level, the degree of commitment, the number of ideas, and the directive style that manifested themselves in the early years of Cameron's leadership are impressive by any standard.

In her first few years at Bethany, Cameron was instrumental in the implementation of a number of significant changes. The most dramatic, both concretely and metaphorically, was the redesign of the worship space; under Cameron's direction, it was literally turned around. When Cameron arrived, the sanctuary was structured for the traditional Eucharist in which the priest celebrated with "his" back to the congregation. In accommodating the space requirements of the new liturgical practices, it was decided, with Cameron's significant input, that the whole space needed reworking. The congregation worshiped in the parish hall while the narthex was moved, the worship space was turned around and enlarged, windows were added, and acoustics were redesigned. In short, a spatial revolution took place. The congregation was deeply involved in the renovation, and Cameron directed the changes with the formal approval and active labor of her church. However, it is clear that the direction and a lot of the motivation for the project were hers.

She was also instrumental in redesigning the kitchen at Bethany, a project that was completed prior to the renovation of the worship space. The kitchen is the physical center of the church, and in many ways it is the center of life there as well. Cameron takes obvious delight in showing visitors the changes that transformed the old, badly constructed space into the warm functional center it is now.

In addition to the physical changes, Cameron instituted a number of new programs, many of which are still ongoing. She encouraged and helped to expand Bethany's inclusivity with regard to membership. This was not a new commitment on the part of many Bethany members but they had not incorporated it in any significant degree prior to Cameron's tenure. She hired a woman assistant who was ordained a deacon and then a priest and who has had two babies while she has served the congregation there.[24] Cameron also became active at the diocesan level around several social justice issues.

According to diocesan guidelines, Cameron was eligible for a three-month sabbatical in 1990 but postponed the leave due to the addition of new staff and her desire to be present during the first liturgical year in the newly renovated church. By 1991, the number and magnitude of these changes, and the speed with which they took place, began to take their toll. Cameron and her congregation

shared a sense of drained resources, and with her church's blessing and support, Cameron took her three-month sabbatical outside
of Atlanta during the fall of 1991. It was a healthy decision and activity both for her and for her church, and she returned with a commitment to take better care of herself and with the confidence that
her church could function just fine while she did so.

To make explicit what has been implicit in the foregoing account, Cameron's leadership style was very directive. Some people
with whom we spoke appreciated the degree of involvement she
had with the activities of the church and experienced her oversight
as expressing caring and concern. Others were more troubled by
her style and experienced it as controlling and manipulative. Whatever one's reaction, during the time of our research Cameron
seemed to be everywhere and to be involved in everything that was
going on at the church. While she spoke of becoming more aware
of the need to place and maintain some clear boundaries between
her professional and personal life, this area constitutes an ongoing
struggle for her.

We will revisit the question of the interplay of gender and leadership in other contexts. For now, I want simply to note that with
the removal of institutional barriers to her priesthood, Cameron
functions as a dynamic, directive, and effective leader in the parish
setting. Personal qualities such as warmth, humor, and intelligence
combine with the authority of the Episcopal priesthood and result
in a nearly perfect fit between this powerful woman and this powerful position. Any reservations that may have initially focused on
her being "the first woman rector" have long since been overcome
by her effectiveness in that role.[25]

The Rector and the Laity

There is no doubt in anyone's mind that Bethany got the strong
leader it was looking for. The question that confronted us as we
observed worship, meetings, and social gatherings is, What happened to the strong, steady lay leadership that guided the church
through the troubling tenure of Cameron's predecessor and the
equally difficult period of transition between rectors? How did that
cadre of leaders respond to this strong rector? What sort of leadership, if any, were they providing?

Our initial impression was that the best way to characterize the
relationship of the laity to the rector was one of dependency.
Cameron seemed to run everything. In conversations with us and
with other church members, Cameron herself frequently voiced the
concern that persons were not "holding up their end" of whatever

program or project they were involved with. She verbalized a need for other people to take more responsibility for the day-to-day life of the church, but it seemed to us that she undermined her own goal by so closely overseeing every aspect of that day-to-day life.

Many of the persons who had assumed formal leadership roles prior to Cameron's coming continued to exercise those roles in the church and new persons joined their ranks. As had been the case prior to Cameron's arrival, there is a startling flexibility in what we might ordinarily think of as gender roles; women function as senior wardens and heads of stewardship campaigns, men cook the meals and do some child care, and vice versa. Thus lay leadership does not organize itself in terms of gender; it seems rather to be almost entirely a function of persons' ability and willingness to commit time and energy to the work of the church. Many of these are the same persons who had done so prior to Cameron's arrival.

And yet, what we thought we were seeing was a highly talented, very directive, even controlling rector and a largely contented, though seemingly dependent, congregation. As I stated above, the rumblings that we heard about Cameron seemed to have more to do with some bruises from her forceful personality than with any deep discontent over her leadership. The church was clearly healthy and happy. Membership was growing, the budget was in better shape—finally catching up with all the improvement projects Bethany had undertaken—programs were flourishing, and Cameron was clearly in charge.

The profile of the church that was clearly emerging just did not fit with our initial impressions of Cameron's leadership at Bethany. In fact, we learned that our initial picture was inaccurate in some key ways. The lay leadership was functioning more subtly but just as powerfully as Cameron was. A crisis in the church created a window that allowed us to look more deeply into the life of Bethany Episcopal Church and to see beyond the forceful leadership style of this rector and the apparent dependency of her congregation into the more subtle exercise of power and authority at the heart of the church. That is the story for our next chapter.

NOTES

1. "Julia" is not her real name. As noted above, all names of persons and churches except those of the author and researchers are pseudonyms.
2. Merry Porter's interview with Julia.
3. The Bethany *Star,* the church newsletter, 7 July 1993.
4. Mary Sudman Donovan, *A Different Call: Women's Ministries in*

the Episcopal Church, 1850–1920 (Wilton, Conn.: Morehouse-Barlow, 1986): 6.

5. For readers not familiar with the language of church architecture, the narthex could be described as the entry hall of the church.

6. Merry Porter, the research assistant for Bethany, was fondly called "the spy," and my title was "chief spy" or "head of the CIA."

7. A senior warden is the head, or chairperson, of the Vestry.

8. My brief historical outline is largely derived from the "official" history of Bethany that was compiled by a longtime Bethany member. He completed his text in 1958 in honor of the church's first sixty years and updated it for its ninetieth birthday. Like a family history written by a proud descendent, this history is filtered through lenses thick with affection, and some of Bethany's warts are thereby rendered opaque. We, of course, supplemented this document with others and with oral histories provided by other longtime Bethany members. However, I do want to acknowledge our debt to and gratitude for this history.

9. From the first page of the church history, not copyrighted.

10. The full name of the national organization was "The Women's Auxiliary to the Domestic and Foreign Missionary Society." It had diocesan and parochial organizations, and within a parish, the subgroups were called Guilds.

11. Dr. Jacobs was named rector emeritus from 1971 until his death in 1975.

12. His letter of resignation is included in the History, 59.

13. History, 60.

14. Dr. Jacobs was generally addressed and referred to as such while Don McGee was almost always called by his first name. I am adopting those practices here.

15. Interview with parishioner, June 1994. Most of the interviewees will remain anonymous in order to protect confidentiality. In those cases in which confidentiality is not an issue, names will be used.

16. The degree of pain experienced by members of the congregation when the rector was forced to leave is articulated well by one of the people we interviewed: "What it felt like was going through the death and the days in the tomb and being told you had to leave when the resurrection was happening." Interview with a parishioner, February 1993.

17. Cameron was not the first priest called by the Vestry at Bethany. The first candidate chosen declined the call. At that point, the committee virtually started over, solicited recommendations for candidates, and it was at this point that Cameron came to Bethany's attention.

18. That statement needs to be qualified by the nature of the authority invested in an Episcopal priest, authority that comes with the ordination to priesthood and is not relinquished even in the face of somewhat ineffective leadership. I will discuss below the deeply

Episcopal nature of Bethany and some of the ways this affects perceptions and practices of power and authority in that church.

19. The phrase is taken from an interview with a parishioner, February 1993.

20. Interview with a parishioner, February 1993.

21. One of the priests who led services in the interim period was a woman. She may have helped to prepare the congregation for reception of a female rector, though she did not spend much time at Bethany. She clearly was not objectionable.

22. History, 76.

23. Merry Porter's interview with Julia.

24. Lisa had been a seminarian at Bethany, and when it was suggested that she might be hired as a part-time deacon, any concerns about having two female priests were overshadowed by the respect and affection the congregation already had for her. Her gender just was not an issue.

25. Some recent sociological research shows that when a woman is an authorized leader, the role has more influence, and even overshadows the influence of gender, in interactions with others. Our small sample and more qualitative research project led us to the same results, as this and following chapters suggest. See Cathryn Johnson, "Gender and Formal Authority," *Social Psychology Quarterly,* 56 (1993): 193–210 and Cathryn Johnson, "Gender, Legitimate Authority, and Leader-Subordinate Conversations," *American Sociological Review,* 59 (February 1994): 122–135.

3 Seeing below the Surface

Priestly Power

Cameron Clark is the strong, powerful leader that Bethany Episcopal Church wanted and needed. As we observed and began to interpret her leadership and its impact on the understandings and practices of power and authority in her church, we quickly encountered institutional interpretations of priestly power and authority. The influence that Cameron has over virtually every aspect of church life in her parish has to be examined in light of Episcopal polity.[1]

There are many complex, intricate issues of clerical authority in the Episcopal Church, and I will note only two. First, a priest is thought to be the embodiment and icon of Christ, and the spiritual authority of the priest is passed down through the "apostolic succession," which is not just a historical pedigree but a claim regarding embodiment of the apostolic faith as proclaimed by the contemporary church.[2] The priest, then, has a different status from the laity. Let me hasten to add that that status is not necessarily considered better, or more Christian; all persons are called and set aside as disciples of Jesus Christ by virtue of their baptism. Second, the priest's spiritual authority conferred through ordination is coupled with the liturgical authority to officiate at the Eucharist, or service of Holy Communion, and other sacrmental functions of the church.[3] Thus there are functional distinctions between priests and the laity that take on great import in a liturgically centered denomination.

For persons who are not members of a sacramental, liturgical tradition, it is difficult to grasp the extent to which the life of the congregation is centered at the communion table. In the first chapter I alluded to the diffuse nature of Bethany's identity, and we saw some elements of that in the last chapter as it appears in the diversity of the congregation, the fluidity of gender roles throughout the church, and the sheer multiplicity of programs and events. In the first chapter I also alluded to constraints on the diffuseness of the identity of this congregation, and in a discussion of the Eucharist we reach the contours of those constraints.

The life of this church is centered in the Eucharist. Liturgial practice provides its identity, for that center provides an anchor in the present, a connection to the past, and a direction for the future. In the absence of such a prominent liturgical center, churches may have to articulate or develop a narrative that provides some continuity for identity: a social justice church, perhaps, or a neighborhood church. We will encounter a form of narrative identity when we turn to St. Matthew's Presbyterian Church. For Bethany, however, such a narrative is not necessary to its identity; a general "Christian narrative" is embodied in its liturgical practice.[4] Bethany's eclectic history, its diverse congregation, its lack of a narrative center does not leave a void but rather functions to create space for newness and growth. Bethany members can be different from one another, can embrace idiosyncracies, can venture into new programmatic territory, because the common core is the Eucharist.[5]

Insofar as the priest is set aside by ordination to perform the priestly tasks, and especially the task of officiating at the sacrament of Holy Communion, the priest has a kind of power and authority not available to the laity. Thus what looked to us like dependency of the congregation on this very energetic and directive rector is in part to be explained by the subtle but nonetheless powerful deference that is accorded an Episcopal priest *qua* priest.

Cameron's gender is nicely accommodated in the priestly role. In the last chapter I will discuss in some detail the role of these senior ministers' gender in the understandings and practices of power and authority in their congregations, and I will bracket that conversation for now. What I do want to point out here is that the parental language and imagery of priesthood is easily adapted across genders, at least in this case.

More than one parishioner told us that "Bethany has a mother." In addition to Cameron's leadership style described in the last chapter—her attentive and thorough oversight of the day-to-day life of the church—she carries other traits and exhibits other behaviors that lend themselves to the characterization of her as mother (though to my knowledge no one actually calls her that in direct address). First, many of her sermons contain anecdotes from her own family of origin; this characteristic of her preaching style was mentioned by some of the parishioners we interviewed, and we ourselves observed it.[6] Cameron is unmarried; we heard lots of stories about her mother, who died in 1984, her father, who had recently moved to Atlanta, and her two sisters. Her own use of family discourse in both literal and metaphorical ways enables such conversation among members of the congregation. Family issues are prominent, and persons seem to feel very free to speak of them. Second, Cameron is comfortable with feelings, their expression, their examination, and their resolution. Again, that, and the presence of many professors, social workers, and therapists as members of the congregation, enable a high level of affective expression and discussion at Bethany. Third, if I had to identify the behavior that is the most characteristic of Cameron's priesthood, I would say without hesitation it is her love for and inclusion of children in all aspects of the church life. After the recessional, children go to her at the back of the church; it is not at all unusual for her to greet congregants with an infant or toddler in her arms. Her office is full of art by children; the church's main stairwell is covered with a mural of animals and plants that was drawn by an adult but painted by, and for, the children. An ongoing challenge, both for Cameron and her congregation, is the best, most effective and most comfortable way to include young children in worship. Excluding them is not an option. Finally, the physical and spiritual space of Bethany centers around two tables: the Holy Communion table in the sanctuary and the big kitchen table where food is prepared. As I noted in the last chapter, men and women officiate at both,[7] and familial language flows.

The power and authority of the priesthood, the dynamic leadership style and deeply nurturing nature of this rector, the easily adapted parental imagery and discourse, all lend themselves to the characterization of Bethany as a family with a strong mother in charge. What the focus issue taught us is that that picture has to be modified by a level of mutuality, interdependence, and general vulnerability that were initially not available for our observation.

The Diagnosis Is AIDS

As part of my series of staff interviews, I had made an appointment to have lunch with the organist, John Bates, on Friday, 15 January 1993. I knew John, of course, but I had not yet spent time listening to his viewpoint on and experience of Bethany. I wanted to do so because he was not only the organist and music director, he was also going to start working part-time in the office, and I thought he would have an interesting perspective on people and events at the church.

I arrived just about on time for our meeting at a local restaurant, and I went inside to wait. After about thirty minutes filled with the usual anxieties in such a situation (Am I at the right restaurant? Is this the right day?) I ate a hurried lunch and left as I had appointments that afternoon.

I did not call John since I did have a busy afternoon, and the weekend flew by. I was in my office on Monday when he called, and he was deeply apologetic about missing our appointment. He said he had felt just terrible and thought he had the flu. I told him to feel better, and after he was well, we would schedule another lunch. The next thing I heard was that John had been diagnosed with pneumonia; I then learned that John had AIDS.

The story of how the news of John's illness was received and disseminated by Cameron and lay leaders in the congregation enables us to see pools and eddies of power and authority that only the management of a crisis will reveal.[8] It began like this: on Monday night, after John had been out with the "flu" for eight days, including two Sundays, John's partner told Cameron that John was "having a little trouble breathing." Learning that John had not seen a doctor (and had no personal physician in Atlanta), Cameron checked to see whether her doctor would see John on an emergency basis. She would, and John's partner Alex made John an appointment the next day. The doctor immediately admitted John to the hospital, and on Friday the diagnosis confirmed what the type of pneumonia suggested: John had AIDS.

At that point, the only other person at Bethany who knew the nature of John's illness was Lisa, the assistant rector. Lisa and John are very close friends, and Lisa and Cameron spent considerable amounts of time with John and his family; they alternated visiting days the entire time John was in the hospital. Lisa and Cameron have a good personal and professional relationship, and both women are likewise deeply fond of John. The two women were able to share their initial reactions to the terrible news and to share the pastoral care for John at this critical time.

Cameron was, of course, very upset to learn than John had a disease that would prematurely end his life. As she said later, her staff is like her family in many ways, a claim that the dynamics of the church bear out. And one of her beloved was diagnosed with a fatal illness. She felt it all.

She was, however, still the rector, and her personal pain could not be allowed to incapacitate her. She had to honor John's request to keep his illness confidential for the time being, and she had to think of how and to what degree to involve the congregation in this tragedy regarding one of their beloved staff members. On the

Sunday after John was diagnosed with AIDS and with his apparent support and consent, Cameron arranged to meet with the outgoing senior warden and the incoming senior warden, both long-term church members and close colleagues of Cameron. (In fact, the incoming senior warden was senior warden when Cameron was hired.) She told them of John's illness and began to talk about ways to disseminate the news to the congregation. Her idea was to write a letter that would be mailed to the church membership so that rumors about John's illness could be supplanted by the truth and so that Cameron could give them pastoral direction to ease their fears about how to respond to John.

It seemed to us that the plan was vintage Cameron. The few days that only she and Lisa knew of the diagnosis left her several steps ahead of her lay leadership in terms of thinking about how to deal with the situation. She engaged in a consultative process that involved her presenting her ideas to people who had not had a chance to process the situation—and I include John in this category—and who agreed that hers was the best approach. She and the two senior wardens spent a lot of time that week writing and rewriting drafts, "50,000 versions," as one participant characterized their attempt to get the letter just right. They passed the drafts around to one another and to John, and generally expended a great deal of energy worrying about and trying to plan for the reactions of others.

Cameron was also very concerned to protect John, and the letter was drafted with that as the primary goal. She was not concerned so much with the need to protect him against viciousness but rather against well-intentioned but exhausting solicitousness.[9] She assumed the role of protective mother quickly and almost without thinking.

The professionalism of her approach with its compassion for John, her concern to help her congregation deal with the reality of AIDS in its midst, her high energy level in drafting and redrafting the letter—all are characteristic of the leadership style that we had seen throughout the life of the church. The two wardens seemed simply to go along with Cameron, giving her feedback but definitely following her lead.

This time, however, we were able to observe a situation in which her expertise was challenged, and lay leadership took over the direction of the process in ways that Cameron welcomed and that showed the quiet but ever-present power and authority that resides in the congregation at Bethany Episcopal Church.

All that the congregation had been told about John was that he was hospitalized with pneumonia, that he was released from intensive care, and that he could receive calls and mail, though he was still too sick to receive many visitors. At this point, Cameron could confide only in Lisa and in the two senior wardens. However, a retreat had been scheduled for the new Vestry for the last weekend in January; that provided the perfect opportunity, with John's consent, for Cameron to tell them what was going on, to enlist their support, and to present the plan regarding the all-church letter.

The retreat started Friday evening at a lovely Episcopal retreat center in the mountains north of Atlanta. Because persons were arriving and leaving at various times, the only time all Vestry members could be present was on Saturday afternoon. That is when Cameron told them about John's illness and the plans to send the letter that she distributed for review and critique.

There were two reactions: dismay at the news of John's diagnosis and concern about plans to inform the congregation. The dismay was manifested initially by a kind of stunned silence. Cameron had been carrying the burdensome knowledge that John had AIDS with few confidants, and she looked forward to telling the rest of the leadership and getting their emotional support and advice. Perhaps it was the group setting of a new Vestry forming itself into a working body; perhaps it was normal unwillingness to take in right away information that we do not really want to have. For whatever reason, most of the group was unable to react immediately, and it took awhile for persons to be able to share their feelings with one another. The sharing did happen, however, and it included Cameron's own vulnerability and her willingness to be open about her pain and her need for their support for her and one another, as well as for John. She allowed herself to be very open about her emotions with this group of persons; they by and large responded with their own pain in a difficult but mutually supportive and honest process.

As a part of that process, there were strong objections both to the style and to the content of the then current plan for the letter. One of the Vestry members, an openly gay man and a close personal friend of Cameron's, was outspoken in his anger that John apparently had so little real control of the situation. He believed that John was much too sick to make the decision that he was supposedly making. This Vestry member was also angry that AIDS was being singled out for special treatment in the way that it was. If John

had had cancer, no one would have planned the letter that had occupied so much of Cameron's and the wardens' time and energy
the week before.

The letter was never sent. Cameron consulted another Episcopal priest who had more experience dealing with AIDS in the congregation. John was given more time, and more room, to make his
own decisions regarding whom to tell and how. Cameron was re-
lieved by and receptive to a more knowledgeable approach to the
reality of a beloved colleague who would live with AIDS and the
communal dimension of that reality. Her own pain and vulnerability did not have to be swallowed up in the busyness of announcements but could rest with others in the hurting.

Both this rector and these lay leaders, including the two wardens, welcomed the genuinely collegial process of caring for one
another and the church—together. A situation that could have
become a power play, a tug-of-war of crisis management, instead
provided the opportunity for genuinely mutual ministry. The lay
leadership challenged the proposed plan of the rector when it
seemed ill-conceived, and it moved gracefully to the rector's side
as vulnerability and responsibility were shared by all.

When John returned to work, he himself told the choir of his
diagnosis, and they responded in love and respect; the rehearsal
went forward that evening with special tenderness. At the rector
and Vestry's suggestion, some laypersons were in contact with
other congregants for whom there was concern that the reality of
AIDS would be especially difficult. John himself has dealt with his
illness with grace and with humor, joking after he got back to work
that the church does not have to spend its money on his pension
plan since he is not likely to need it. John is a gentle, quiet man. It
is his style that is setting the pace in this instance; both the rector
and the church have made way for him.

Looking through the Window

Our initial impressions of Cameron Clark's leadership as rector
of Bethany Episcopal Church were modified and deepened by our
observation of the power and authority of the lay leaders in this
episode of crisis in the life of the church, its members, and its rector. We were puzzled by what seemed to be an incommensurate
mix of a controlling rector and the playfulness and informality of
the congregation's life. We were unable to make sense of what
were clearly indications of mutuality and interdependence when all
we could see on the surface was a rector who was firmly in charge
of everything.

What we were able to see in this very painful series of episodes as the rector and the lay leadership struggled to deal personally and corporately with a beloved member's diagnosis of AIDS was the layer of interdependence and mutuality that functions in the life of Bethany. There is no question about Cameron's power and authority as priest; she and Lisa and other priests officiate at the practice that constitutes the heart of the congregation's life, the Eucharist. As important as the kitchen table is at Bethany, and as representative as it is of the fluid roles at the church, the communion table is the undisputed center of the community's life. The family metaphors that are so easily invoked when one observes the activities and interactions of the congregation at Bethany are more complex than they might at first seem. Cameron is mother, but she is also sister, and perhaps on occasion, even daughter. Her role requires boundaries between her personal and her professional life that are a constant struggle for her to maintain. However, in terms of the leadership of the church apart from the communion table, there is both the possibility and the reality of more mutuality and interdependence than Cameron's style at first suggested to us. When the issues are not deemed especially important by the congregants, or when they are deemed important and Cameron's insight and energy are compelling, as with the rearrangement of the worship space, the authority of the laity operates to support her direction. However, that authority is not passive, and when her direction is questionable, or when the issue or situation evokes a counter-energy in laypersons, genuine collaboration and negotiation take place.

In an interview with Lisa, the assistant rector, she observed that the power and authority she has as a priest in that place is partly dependent upon the power and authority the people give her. The priesthood carries with it the presumption of power and authority; she remarked that there are some people for whom a priest seems to do no wrong. However, she said, "I think in this parish, power is not authoritarian." I interpret her statement to mean that power is characterized by interdependence, effectiveness, and a desire for the well-being of everyone. Our study showed her to be right. Even with the power conveyed by the priesthood, the power and authority of the priests at Bethany are in part a negotiated reality.[10]

Issues of Structure

So far our discussion has focused largely on personal and interpersonal issues of power and authority. It is also important to note that the fluid leadership structure and the general inclusiveness of the congregation that stands as background and support to that structure are very important elements in the dynamics and the management of all congregational issues.

What we encountered at Bethany Episcopal Church is a fascinating mix of hierarchical clerical authority and largely egalitarian lay authority with both facets present in the interactions between clergy and laity. The Episcopal Church is structured along classic hierarchical lines, and Cameron challenges those lines only occasionally. For example, she will use inclusive language in her own prayers and sermons, but she will not alter one word of the liturgy. By her very presence as a priest and rector, she upsets some old and cherished notions about who can and should embody the hierarchy, and she functions as a part of it in her position in the parish and in her work with and on behalf of the diocese. In the common language of virtually all Episcopal clergy, her assistant rector, Lisa, serves "at the pleasure . . . of the rector," a phrase that Cameron quotes to her with mischievious glee, and Lisa is content with that definition.[11] John's role is defined in terms of the music programs of the church, and he too is content to have Cameron be boss. As we have seen, her own personality and leadership style work well with the degree of official authority that she has.

There is also a hierarchy of the laity, of sorts, as the Vestry takes leadership roles over various aspects of the life of the congregation and assumes the commensurate responsibility. Those areas of responsibility are defined and distributed at the beginning of each Vestry's term. This is a practice that Cameron initiated, and it is now well known that being on the Vestry is not a figurehead role. Thus people who are Vestry members are usually those who are willing to commit time and energy to the congregational life of their parish. Other church groups, such as the Episcopal Church Women, have officers, and in some cases the leadership of those subsidiary groups is held by a small number of persons over the years. However, at this church, the boundaries between lay leaders and others is extremely permeable, and lay leadership really is a matter of commitment and energy on the part of individual members. There is a deeply egalitarian strain in the congregation as a whole with leadership roles being unconnected from factors such as gender, age, occupation, and social and economic resources. Nonleadership roles such as coffee-hour groups and Christian education programs are also open and fluid.

As we saw during the crisis of John's diagnosis with AIDS and various negotiations for deciding on a response, there is also a strong interdependence between the clergy and the laity. Power and authority shifted according to the criterion of expertise; knowledge trumped position. The focus issue has allowed us to see how far the understanding and practice of power and authority have shifted at Bethany since Dr. Jacobs's tenure; he settled conflict and change by pronouncement, whereas Cameron was grateful for the shared responsibility and vulnerability between her and the Vestry.

As a feminist, it has been very instructive for me to watch this blend of hierarchy and egalitarianism. Feminist analysis may sometimes dismiss hierarchy as intrinsically sexist without paying nuanced attention to the scope of its function and authority.[12] Not all hierarchies are oppressive, and it seems that in this church at this time, hierarchy functions very nicely alongside deep and pervasive egalitarian power and authority. The alliance is fragile, of course, and depends in part upon Cameron's desire to share power and authority with her congregation. If there were a more authoritarian leader, or even a more ineffectual one, the egalitarian nature of congregational life might recede. One can only speculate, however, and hypothesis gives way to concrete, lived experience in this instance in this time and place.[13]

At another level, the egalitarian elements of the understanding and practice of power and authority are to be understood against the background of and as part of a commitment to an inclusive church. I introduced above the fact that Bethany is committed to inclusivity; it is time to discuss in greater detail the effects of that commitment on issues of power and authority.

Bethany Episcopal Church has a largely white membership, and that fact has to be seen in the context of a city (and no doubt also a whole society) that is still deeply divided along racial lines, certainly in religious institutions. However, as a white church, Bethany's commitment and practice are inclusive.

Demographically, it is not dramatically different from other, less inclusive churches. In terms of the life of the church, however, everyone is welcome everywhere. Most activities are intergenerational, and the generations really interact. I have already remarked several times about the central role played by the children of Bethany; persons of all ages interact more freely than I have observed elsewhere. There is also a commitment to including gay men and lesbians as full and integral members, not just on the church rolls but also in the life of the congregation. That commitment has come not without resistance and controversy from some church members, but it has not caused the deep divisions that some churches fear. Persons are not identified by their sexual orientation, necessarily, but same-sex couples attend worship and other events without negative comment. Several leaders of the church are non-heterosexual, and Cameron is clear in her stance that all Christians are welcome.[14]

The inclusivity of the congregation and the egalitarian element in the congregational life are the context in which we must view the open negotiations around power and authority when John's illness became known. The interdependence in that instance between this strong leader and her congregation was not an anomaly. The interdependence is an ongoing reality of congregational life that is at times rendered invisible by Cameron's forceful personality and by her liturgical priestly power and authority, but which is quietly operative and always available to draw on when necessary.

As a kind of footnote to this account, it must be said that Bethany Church, including its clergy, was in a good position to respond with compassion and support to a staff member with AIDS because of the life they already shared. It may be the case that a congregation that is not inclusive could somehow rally with a positive response, but it is hard to imagine that it could happen with the grace and clarity of the response at Bethany. There was from the outset a shared goal: everyone wanted what was best for John. The controversy and conflict that I have recorded were only about strategies for effecting that goal, not about the goal itself.[15] Bethany did not experience controversy regarding a staff member with AIDS, and that fact was a blessing to all concerned.

I began my discussion of Bethany Episcopal Church by recalling a worship service in which Julia Jacobs was received as a deacon in the Episcopal Church. In that act, the church officially recognized the ministry of one to whom the upper levels of the hierarchy had been closed because of her gender. We have seen the powerful leadership of a woman to whom the hierarchy opened its doors and who functions so effectively within it. And through all this, we have seen the power of the laity to negotiate with the priest on the basis of expertise and guidance, and we have seen the authority of lay leaders to work with the priest on behalf of the life of the church. The picture is complex, lively, and dynamic.

The intriguing blend of hierarchical and egalitarian elements, the sharing of power and authority according to activity and need among clergy and laity, the close ties between responsibility and energy, and the playfulness that we have noted all characterize the life of this congregation. It is now time to look at another vibrant church with a very different nature and very different understandings and practices of power and authority.

NOTES

1. The official document of the polity of the Episcopal Church is the *Constitution and Canons for the Government of the Protestant Episcopal Church in the United States of America Otherwise Known As The Episcopal Church*. The General Conventions, 1991.
2. The question of embodiment of authority was, of course, a prominent issue in controversies surrounding the ordination of women. The literature on that topic is vast. For a balanced, historical summary of the arguments see Michael McFarlene Marrett, *The Lambeth Conferences and Women Priests: The Historical Background of the Conferences and Their Impact on the Episcopal Church in America* (Smithtown, N.Y.: Exposition Press, 1981).
3. See the *Canons,* especially Title III, Canon 14, 80–82.
4. The extent to which the identity of Christian congregations, and Christian identity itself, is narrative-dependent is a complex issue of another order from the one I am developing here. Surely liturgical practices are themselves somehow reflective of the story of Jesus Christ and the people who call him "the Christ," but how that relationship is constituted is a debatable issue. All I am pointing to is that the particular story of a particular church can lack cohesion without a loss of identity in the presence of a sacramental center.
5. One of my favorite comments was from a congregant who was talking about some of the more outstanding characters at Bethany. She said gleefully, "Down here in the South we put our crazy folks on the front porch and call them family." I don't know about how generally that applies to southern churches, but it certainly is true of Bethany.
6. This characteristic of her preaching gets mixed reviews, with the approval outweighing the disapproval.
7. The bishop, of course, celebrated the Eucharist, and there was a male priest on staff part-time.
8. In deciding to use this series of incidents to illustrate the more subtle interactions between Cameron and her congregation, and among the congregants themselves, I gave serious thought to the potentially exploitive nature of such a choice. I consulted with Letty Russell, who was an advisor to the research project and who herself helped to write a book titled *The Church with AIDS* (Louisville, Ky.: Westminster John Knox Press, 1990). I consulted, of course, with Cameron, and it was she who raised the issue with John about using the management of his illness as an illustration here. I spoke with John, too, about his agreement to be discussed

in this way. I admit to some lingering reservations. They have been overcome by our hope that Bethany's experience may prove useful for other congregations who will have to make decisions about persons with AIDS in their midst. Again, this discussion is not about persons with AIDS, per se, but rather about how the handling of the news of John's diagnosis reveals the negotiation and use of power and authority in that church.

9. Cameron is quick to acknowledge that her proposals in this regard grew directly out of her experience of being exhausted by well-meaning church members in another parish where she served at the time that her mother was dying. She wanted to protect John (and herself?) from the draining effects of incessant sympathy.

10. In a widely cited study from the field of social psychology, Morris Zelditch, Jr., and Henry A. Walker argue that the "consensual" aspect of the legitimation of power in group settings is at least as much a function of a "collective process of social validation" as it is dependent upon each individual's conscious consent. Thus the assumption of authority by a group is an important aspect of anyone's exercise of that authority. On the other hand, individuals and groups of individuals can withdraw from and/or dissent from that process, and authority is undermined. Their work provides at least the skeleton of an interesting phenomenology of consent to power. Morris Zelditch, Jr., and Henry A. Walker, "Legitimacy and the Stability of Authority," in *Advances in Group Processes,* vol. 1, (J.A.I. Press, 1984), 1–25.

11. I specifically asked Lisa in an interview how her role was officially defined. She explained it and referred me to the *Canons*. In an attempt not to project my own feelings about this arrangement, I also asked Lisa how she felt about it. She said that she might want her own parish someday, but for now she was happy with her role at Bethany.

12. Some of the early literature in feminist theology tended toward a rejection of hierarchical arrangements as inherently oppressive. See Rosemary Radford Ruether, *Sexism and God-Talk: Toward a Feminist Theology* (Boston: Beacon Press, 1983). A more nuanced approach can be found in Letty Russell's suggestion of the practice of shifting roles among members of a community and an emphasis on service to the marginalized; see Letty Russell, *Church in the Round: Feminist Interpretation of the Church* (Louisville, Ky.: Westminster John Knox Press, 1993). Our observations suggest an even more complex and comfortable juxtaposition of hierarchical and egalitarian authority structures.

13. In fact, the history of Bethany suggests that when the clerical leadership is ineffective for one reason or another, the lay leadership, whoever that may be at the time, works well to keep the church functioning.

14. When AIDS was first discovered and means of transmission were

uncertain, some communicants began to intinct, that is, to dip the wafer in the chalice of wine rather than touching the edge of the chalice with their lips for a sip. Cameron was unsympathetic with their concern since transmission through communion had been deemed well nigh impossible by leading authorities. However, when John's AIDS became known and it became paramount for persons with AIDS to be able to receive communion without getting any infections from the chalice, she reversed herself. Currently, at the invitation to Holy Communion, intinction is mentioned as an option for any who wish it.

15. Even at Bethany, some of the lay leaders of the church met with a few individual parishioners to tell them about John's diagnosis and to diffuse any rejection that might be forthcoming. The numbers were very small, and Cameron never had to get directly involved in that aspect of the crisis. There was certainly nothing resembling factions within the church.

4   A Maverick Church

Welcome to St. Matthew's

Like the area of the city in which it is located, the twenty-five acres of St. Matthew's "campus" embody opulence, abundance, and serene beauty. Even the trees surrounding the parking lot of St. Matthew's Presbyterian Church extend a gracious invitation to member and visitor alike, and I felt both welcomed and somewhat intimidated as I walked toward the church building on a lovely Sunday morning. When I rounded the corner and climbed the steps to the outside portico, I was greeted by several people I imagined as "pillars of the church." I later realized the six men were ushers, all dressed in suits and ties, tall, dignified, late middle-aged, sturdy-looking and, well, pillarlike. There were women mingling and greeting elsewhere on the porch and the narthex, but these stately men were my welcoming committee that day.

The sanctuary of St. Matthew's is beautiful; the Greek revival style of the exterior with its addition of a Christopher Wren-style steeple is even more impressive on the inside with its arched windows and columns and lovely, molded ceiling, all painted white.[1] Though it is not huge by Southern Presbyterian standards, the church feels spacious and is impeccably designed. I had the sense that nothing in that place was out of place or there by happenstance.

Persons filed into the sanctuary from the back, as I had, and from the front through two doors on either side of the chancel. There was the usual bustling and gentle conversation of a congregation gathering for worship, with words often punctuated by restrained laughter. The gathering time managed to be both warm and formal.

As I watched people enter and take their seats, I was struck by the appearance of the members; I had the visual impression of remarkable homogeneity—persons garbed in the "St. Matthew's uniform," as we soon came to call it.[2] While there were some definite dress codes at work—not one woman wore pants on this particular Sunday, and I did not see an open-collared shirt on a man—the sense of sameness of dress among the attendees was attributable to good grooming as much as to the similarity of particular items of clothing. Like the building itself, the congregation was carefully put together. No one and nothing was mussed, and it was hard to imagine that they ever were. Finally, the entire congregation was white, except for one black couple in the back, whom we later learned was from Africa and was being sponsored by St. Matthew's.

One of the outstanding features of the worship life of St. Matthew's—some would say the heart of its worship—is the music. The organ prelude was breathtaking, and its concert quality is no accident. The organist and choir director of St. Matthew's plays with the Atlanta Symphony Orchestra, and many of the choir members are part of the Atlanta Symphony choral programs. Furthermore, the acoustics, either by design or chance, not only enhance the sounds from the chancel but swallow sound in the rest of the sanctuary. Thus congregational singing is muffled, whereas even soft solos from the chancel are clearly audible. The music is overwhelmingly baroque, and worship at St. Matthew's is, in part, a concert.

There is an acolyte to light the candles at the communion table.[3] Otherwise, there is no lay participation in the liturgy of worship, except, of course, for the professional-sounding choir. Clergy staff of the church perform all liturgical roles, including scripture reading, prayer, announcements, and offering. The service as a whole is flawless, with none of the awkward moments that can so painfully call attention away from worship and to the efforts to structure worship. The service flows unimpeded.

The grounds, the buildings, the congregants, the music, and the liturgy provide an astonishingly congruent experience. It is elegant and professional. Nothing jars or distracts or seems out of place. This is, at least on first impression, a church confident of itself and deeply unified along many dimensions.

In the Beginning

St. Matthew's was founded in 1949 as a church to serve the new neighborhood that was developing in northwest Atlanta, and from its beginning it provided a number of important and self-conscious contrasts to other Southern Presbyterian churches, even in metropolitan Atlanta. In the first place, it could be said to be almost an accident that the church is Presbyterian, rather than some other

Christian Protestant denomination. It grew not out of the vision and fervor of some minister or group of believers of any one denomination but out of the needs of a growing and sophisticated neighborhood into which were migrating many young, very well-educated families who were active participants and leaders in Atlanta's growing postwar economy. The original group was composed of persons from several Protestant denominations and some Jewish families, as well. What they needed, aside from a church in a convenient geographical location, was a place to worship that could embrace the intellectual sophistication, the cultural polish, and the diverse spiritual and theological needs and positions of the people who gathered there.

They found the perfect leader in Carroll Samuelson. He was a southerner educated in the liberal theological tradition of the north; he attended Princeton Theological Seminary, but his thought was most powerfully shaped by the work of Paul Tillich. He valued thoughtfulness above mindless piety, tolerance over creedal conformity, and justice over success, at least as he interpreted those things.

It is not possible to understand St. Matthew's Presbyterian Church or its founding pastor without understanding something of fundamentalist Southern Presbyterianism, at least as it is understood by St. Matthew's members, because it is southern Christian fundamentalism that defines everything St. Matthew's reacts against. The perception, at least, is that Christian fundamentalism is based on a narrow range of theological and ethical convictions that are not to be subjected to intellectual interrogation from other perspectives. It is the perception that when faith and reason are at odds, which they often are, faith wins, even at the cost of anti-intellectualism. It is the perception that lines of human authority are clear, and ideas and convictions come already interpreted and ready to be put into practice without further reflection. It is the perception, at least, that Christian fundamentalism is triumphalist, inward-looking, intellectually shallow, inappropriately emotive, and sometimes silly. It is all those things that St. Matthew's is not and was founded not to be. To use the fundamentalist vernacular, if Christians from St. Matthew's walk and talk with Jesus, they would expect it to be a two-way conversation.

In our interviews with longtime St. Matthew's members, there are three characteristics of the church and of Carroll Samuelson that almost always emerge. The first is the off-center, alternative nature of the church, and the "maverick" nature of its pastor that I just described. In positive terms, St. Matthew's has embodied from the beginning a commitment to excellence in education and the arts in all that it does. People still talk about how intellectually challenging, if often confusing, Rev. Samuelson's sermons were. He did not follow a lectionary; he was as likely to take something from Tillich for his sermon text as he was to preach on a Bible passage, and "bibliolatry" itself was one of his favorite themes. In fact, we were struck by how Tillichian the language at St. Matthew's still sounds. The education program at St. Matthew's has been outstanding through the years, and that tradition is still central to its life. Classes may have a traditional theological focus, but they are as often structured around themes from the fine arts or "new science" as on anything traditionally taught in Christian adult education classes. I have already offered a brief description of the music program. Its excellence is a feature that the present program continues but did not originate and that is part of the St. Matthew's heritage and identity. "Maverick" and "commitment to excellence" were the two most frequent terms of self-identification of this congregation.

The second set of stories that emerges has to do with the bold and very liberal stand the church took during the Civil Rights era in the 1960s. Even its courageous position on social justice was related to the centrality of its commitment to educational excellence. The congregation had started an elementary school that met in the church, and the decision was made in the early 1960s to integrate the school. Carroll Samuelson took a nonnegotiable stand on the matter, as he did on racial integration in general, and he had the support of a number of influential St. Matthew's members, though certainly not all. The integration of St. Matthew's school divided the church, and we are told that several hundred church members left. It was, then, a painful time for the congregation in some ways, but those who stayed recall the period as a formative, and basically healthy, development in the life of the church. Their position on the integration of their own school defined even more clearly a group of people who were affluent but socially progressive and whose identity was a clear alternative to all the elements that were seen as intellectually backward. Many people, including Rev. Samuelson, now pastor emeritus, still speak with pride about the lack of concern over membership numbers and persons' consistent focus on what seemed to them clearly to be the right thing to do. The church remained committed to excellence in education at all levels, and a private, racially integrated elementary school was the embodiment of that commitment even as it continued to characterize the church and its pastor as mavericks in the context of conservative southern Protestantism.

The third set of remembrances about the earlier years of St. Matthew's life as a church is related to Rev. Samuelson's deep affinity and amazing relationships with the children and young adolescents of the church. He is described as rather socially awkward in large groups of adults. With children, however, he was a kind of Pied Piper, with pockets filled with balloons and candy, and a gentle, comfortable way that adults rarely experienced except in one-on-one situations. Several people commented that families sometimes stayed in the church when the adults were dissatisfied with some aspect of church life because the children loved St. Matthew's so deeply and felt so affirmed, even beloved, by its senior pastor.

As we interviewed women in the church, in particular, we kept encountering references to the "Bare Bears," a group founded by Samuelson for seventh-grade girls. He had originally begun a group for older teens, both males and females, and took them on hikes in the mountains of North Georgia and other social outings. As that group died out, he recognized a need among the younger female teens for something special that was just for them. It was his observation that the young adolescent males had lots of opportunities in that social setting to be part of groups, including sports activities, scout activities, and other school-sponsored groups. The preteen girls, however, had fewer choices, as he first learned through the experience of his own daughter's struggling through her twelfth year of life. So Samuelson began the Bare Bears. They went twice a year on overnight excursions; they met at the church between times, and the group functioned as kind of a secret society in which Samuelson gave each girl her own nickname. All of them were bound by the kind of secret rituals that prefigured sorority life. Many of these women who are now adults in the church speak with deep gratitude of that group, and they still will not share their secret names. The group lasted through two generations of Bare Bears in some of the church families. So pivotal a role did this group play in the lives of many female members of St. Matthew's that women who were and are extremely active in the church and who joined under Samuelson's tenure but who were too old to be a Bare Bear speak wistfully even now of feeling excluded from the inner circle, a phrase we heard a lot.

The stories of this group, both from Samuelson himself and from the girls and women who participated in it, offered us the experience of being transported to another age. When the stories began to surface, we were initially very concerned about what we may have unknowingly uncovered, and we asked very direct and probing questions about the possibility that there may have been something abusive or exploitive about this group, its activities, and its relationship to Samuelson. What we discovered, rather, was a reality that helped to shape the identity of a church, that was deeply and lovingly formative in the lives of many of the girls and women, and that would no longer be possible in the age in which we live. In fact, Samuelson speaks very openly about his realization that seventh-grade girls became increasingly sophisticated, and in the process they lost some of the innocence that had characterized the group whom he initially reached. That, in turn, shaped the dynamics of the group in ways that no one individual could transform completely, even a person as powerful as Samuelson was in that church. In this time of youthful sophistication and with the proliferation of instances of clergy sexual abuse, the very aura and expectation of innocence that sometimes protects innocence is absent from our world. In some important respects, then, the experiences of the Bare Bears are no longer available, and even the existence of such a group would be problematic, no matter what the composition of the group was. But the legacy of that innocence, and the deep trust that was not betrayed, is a powerful and important current in the lives of many individual members of St. Matthew's. It is also a part of its identity as a safe and gentle place and as a kind of bastion against harsher forces in the wider world.[4] Ugly and terrible things do not go on at St. Matthew's, and this part of its history confirms the church's self-image.

Congregational Power and Authority

Details about how influence and authority were assigned and functioned at St. Matthew's through the 1960s and 1970s are difficult to retrieve twenty years later. Some things can be said with confidence: Carroll Samuelson was a very powerful man in every aspect of the church in which he wanted to participate, largely because he was trusted so deeply by the congregation to be the pastor. Two features of the organization of St. Matthew's at that time are relevant to that claim. First, one former member described the power arrangement as a wheel with Samuelson as the hub, and all interaction between the spokes went through him. That is not literally true, of course, but as a metaphor it is probably more accurate than not. His position, however, was based on what seem to be two assumptions generally shared by the church members: jobs are done by experts, and lines of authority among the laity are drawn informally and on an ad hoc basis. The former assumption is still operative at St. Matthew's. The congregation's drive toward excellence in everything that it does means that the church is to be

run by those who know how to run churches, that is, by professional staff people. Samuelson was trusted to run the church because he was the pastor and he did get done what needed doing
within the maverick profile that I sketched above. The second assumption, that lines of authority among laypersons are informally
drawn on an as-needed basis has been superseded to some extent
by much more formal structures and systems in the church. This
change occurred in a process that I will begin to outline in the next
section. However, under most of Samuelson's long tenure, he implemented programs and funded projects largely through the informal contacts he had with the persons in the congregation.[5] A
well-timed phone call, a meeting, or a series of quiet conversations
resulted in the job getting done. Again, I want to emphasize that
for most members of the church, that was not thought to be an inappropriate leadership style. The pastor was supposed to lead the
church, and so long as the job got done with efficiency and civil-
ity, most persons were quite content with the process.

Perhaps part of the reason that this potentially alienating lack
of formal structure worked so well was because a lot of people
were involved in the ongoing life of the church. Persons could become active in any area of the church life in which they were interested, and availability of time determined who constituted the
lay leadership at any particular point in the church's history. Thus
access to lay leadership functions was informal but for the most part
not closed. It was also the case that the congregational life of St.
Matthew's could gracefully accommodate the life cycle of availability as young couples would join, be very active, become less involved as growing families and careers demanded more attention,
and then become more active again as other areas of life provided
the necessary openings.

The two kinds of power and authority, then, functioned rather
smoothly together in most cases. Samuelson's "kitchen cabinet" as
some have called it, was summoned or not as the occasions war-
ranted with all important decisions going through Samuelson himself and with his convictions being negotiated into action behind
the scenes. For the most part, these powerful lay members were
wealthy and influential persons in the Atlanta community. Some
were active in the day-to-day life of the church; others apparently
never were.

Alongside that "old boy's" network (all the members of that
group were men) was the day-to-day governance and administrative structure with its open access to any members who had the
time and interest to participate. Most people seem to have been

aware of this layered structure and acquiescent, if not completely comfortable, with the system. It is my impression that the congregation's tolerance of a formal and a more powerful informal authority structure was familiar to them from other areas of their lives, as corporate structures and social clubs of which they were a part operated in a similar fashion. Furthermore, many members of St. Matthew's were willing to "leave their power at the door"[6] when they attended church because they wanted their participation in church to be a respite from the leadership and decision making that characterized so much of the rest of their lives. Many were quite content with passive roles. Even some of those who were not as comfortable remained members of St. Matthew's because so many of their other needs—intellectual, social, and educational—were being met by this unique church.

The Crisis of Leadership

For all its social homogeneity, St. Matthew's was tolerant of and even encouraged a range of intellectual ideas and theological beliefs. (Their theological intolerance extended mainly to intolerance—a part of their legacy of rejecting Southern Protestant fundamentalism.) And for all the power that Samuelson exerted in his congregation, at least on matters of importance to him, the congregation was also capable of dealing with disagreement regarding even central features of its church life. An example of the latter is the controversy over whether to move the school that St. Matthew's founded and ran, and that was such a central and formative part of its identity as a racially inclusive church in the 1960s. Since its beginning, the school had operated on church grounds with direct church oversight. Eventually, a group of persons felt that the school should be moved to another location and be operated with more independence from the church. The major concern motivating this group was that the time and energy required by the school was draining resources, both human and financial, that could better be spent on community service, another deeply held value of St. Matthew's members. Extra Session meetings were called, and the merits and demerits of each proposal were pondered and debated. Feelings ran high, but decorum was maintained. They decided to move the school, and though there were dissenting votes, the congregation was able to support the majority recommendation. Many church members still continue to send their children to St. Matthew's school. They serve on the board and volunteer in various capacities, and the church still provides some financial support. However, this fine private elementary school that still bears the church's name is today a largely independent enterprise. The decision was not easy, and the process of reaching it was difficult, but it was not traumatic.

I offer this account of the decision to move St. Matthew's school as a contrast to the process that church members refer to as "the most painful period in the history of the church." There is no candidate for that title other than the episodes I am about to relate, and people still have difficulty speaking about what happened. There is no one version, of course; that fact reflects the disparate realities that constituted part of the crisis at the time. The account that follows represents a kind of timeline of events. I will relate them in a straightforward and unbiased way, and I will offer at the end an analysis both of the events and of the reason for their explosive and even violent effects on the congregation.

Off and on through Samuelson's time as pastor, St. Matthew's had a series of associate and youth pastors. But such was Samuelson's presence in the church, and the regard with which his leadership was held, that these other ministers are only shadowy and vague references in persons' recollection of their church's past. A layperson was in charge of Christian education; she was serving the penultimate year of her long career at St. Matthew's when we were doing our on-site research. The church's music was in the hands of another layperson, who is said to have ruled it with an iron hand, but she was widely acknowledged as providing an excellent program. These long-term professional staff persons executed their program responsibilities with expertise regarded as appropriate. Youth programs are known to be the weak spot in the St. Matthew's profile of excellence in the past, and one can only speculate on the effect that Samuelson's attachment to and role with the youth had on the problem. In any event, no assistant or associate pastor surfaces in congregants' memories with any clarity or significance.[7]

In the early 1980s the church was looking for an associate again, and not being especially successful. One of the people who had been consulting with the search committee and with others working on the issue was George Lewis. Lewis was a Presbyterian minister who was working for the Atlanta Presbytery, and whose family had joined St. Matthew's in 1979 shortly after they moved to Atlanta from New York. In 1982 during one of his meetings with the search committee, several of the most influential members suggested that the perfect person for the job was George himself. His initial reaction to the suggestion was an unequivocal no. He was happy with his administrative position with the denomination, and his career was too well established for him to consider taking on the role of an associate pastor, even in one of the most outstanding Presbyterian churches in the country. He would be happy to assist their search in any way that he could, but he was surely not himself a candidate for the job.

This group from St. Matthew's was populated with powerful lawyers and businessmen, people who were used to negotiating and making deals. They came back to George and asked what it would require to get his interest in their proposition. Thus began a series of talks, with Carroll Samuelson centrally included by all parties, that resulted in what members refer to as "the copastorate." By at least some accounts of the deal that was struck, George agreed to join the staff at St. Matthew's in 1983 as a copastor with Samuelson, and as such they would have equal power and authority in the organizational composition of the church's life. George and Carroll had spent a lot of time deciding who would oversee what, and it looked as though their different skills and interests would provide a nice combination for the church. Carroll and the church that he had led so long were already contemplating the eventual end to his leadership there, and while there was apparently a wide range of expectations regarding George's role at Carroll's retirement, it was clear that George's work would mark some sort of initial moment of transition for St. Matthew's. Overcoming his original reluctance and with a deal all parties thought would be beneficial, George did join the clergy staff of St. Matthew's in 1983. Carroll had primary responsibility for finance, building and grounds, and for preaching and worship, although George preached regularly as well. George was the minister of congregational life and outreach, including pastoral care, although Carroll participated in pastoral care as well.

At first, by all accounts, things went well, although it is interesting to note that the accounts diverge from this point regarding what actually transpired. Still, for a while this unusual leadership arrangement met the needs of the church and the pastors. Carroll could continue doing what he loved to do without having to get involved in the complexities of instituting and implementing administrative structures for church programs which both the growing size and the changing times of the church were beginning to require.[8] George could create structures for the smooth running of old programs, both within the church and those involved in community outreach, and he could create the possibilities for a greatly expanded number of programs and participants. Both men were involved in the worship life of the church, although worship was so indelibly stamped by Carroll's personality and theological approach that George had more or less to conform to worship as usual. However, respecting the practices and styles of a church's worship is appropriate for a new pastor in any church, and George was a full participant in the worship life of the church. Both men were involved in the pastoral care of the congregation, though with very different styles. Carroll took time to introduce George to certain key people in the church's history and present, and George was interested in the challenges and the culture in which he found himself immersed. Initially, it seemed to be working.

Like an old, silent movie that jerks between scenes, the account moves now to a worship service in the spring of 1987. Carroll made two announcements from the pulpit that morning that shook the congregation. First, he announced the unexpected death the day before of one of the most beloved members of St. Matthew's. Many people did not know of this event, so Carroll's abrupt announcement in church that day was the first they heard of the loss of a man who was not only beloved but deeply influential, both in the church and in the wider community. He was also one of Carroll's closest and most trusted friends, a member of his kitchen cabinet, and a person whose advice had been crucial for many, many years. Carroll's other announcement was that he would retire in two years, in 1989. He had been planning to make the second announcement long before he knew he would have to make the first, but I have often wondered why he insisted on coupling them in one service. Announcing one's retirement two years ahead of the event is not common practice. There surely was no rush. But both announcements were made that day, and the shock in the congregation, the sense of loss and abandonment, must have been intense. Persons recall leaving that service feeling numb.

At this point, accounts of what happened begin to differ widely, though an outline of events still emerges. Sometime in the weeks following Carroll's announcement, a transition team was formed to guide the church through Carroll's retirement and into the next phase. At that point, a number of hitherto submerged tensions regarding the copastorate began to surface, along with wildly disparate expectations of what the arrangement would mean for the future of St. Matthew's. George entered this period with a clear, though as it turns out, undocumented expectation that his participation in the copastorate included his succession to Carroll as the next senior minister of St. Matthew's,[9] and the transition team in fact ended up recommending that. Carroll, on the other hand, though not in any formal way central to the process, expressed serious reservations about such an arrangement, and he was only part of a strong and influential group that strongly opposed George's becoming the next senior pastor. Some of the objections were, no doubt, personal responses to George. However, a significant and widely shared concern had to do with the process itself. It was felt by many that the health of the church required the formal and usual transitional process of having interim ministers, whom everyone knew to be temporary, while it compiled its parish profile and conducted a national search for the best person to lead the church. After forty years, the church would need some time before it would be ready to move on to new leadership.

The two groups came to an impasse. Special Session meetings were called, some with and some without the transition team. All of the possibilities and proposals were presented. And things fell apart.

St. Matthew's had faced disagreement, even controversy regarding issues that church members regarded as central several times in the history of the church, and such situations did not necessarily constitute self-defined crises as we saw in the case of the decision to move the school. Some churches might interpret the decision to integrate St. Matthew's School as a deeply painful time since the decision split the church and resulted in the resignation of several hundred members. St. Matthew's clearly does not; rather the group that stayed saw the outcome as confirmation of its commitment, and the commitment of its pastor, to do what was right, especially in contrast to Southern conservative Presbyterianism. The self-declared, self-defined crisis for St. Matthew's was the hostility that was not only felt but expressed on a number of different levels and in a number of different directions around the copastorate. Anger surfaced and was spoken and was allowed to look ugly. Emotion overcame reason and breeding and gentility, and people at St. Matthew's wounded each other, for they did not pull back before the fight got ugly. Trust was broken, and the effects of the perceived betrayals around the congregation linger like fading scars that occasionally still ache.

The members of St. Matthew's Presbyterian Church do not behave the way they did in 1988–89. These people did not raise their voices or shed tears of anger and humiliation in Session meetings. They did not impugn other people's character in public. They did not air out-of-control emotions, and they did not allow emotions to overcome reasonable discussion. But all that happened, and the accounts of this time still strain and soften the voices of those who relate them. In stories of the copastorate period, remembered pain surfaces like puffs of old dust.

With the church unable to resolve the issue in committee

process, the matter was put to a congregational vote. The vote was 51 percent in favor of having George Lewis succeed Carroll Samuelson as senior pastor. Lewis wisely recognized that that slim majority vote did not constitute the support he needed or wanted, and he resigned.

What happened? Why did the mess begin, and why did they not clean it up before it got so nasty? A number of factors can be identified, though there are no doubt influences and personal dynamics and other reasons that we simply will never know.

In hindsight it is clear that the copastorate experiment was predestined to fail. Both clergy involved now realize that it was not possible for a person to come into a church and share power and authority with someone who was the founding pastor and who had been there nearly forty years, no matter how talented and experienced the second man was. I think it is fair to say that both men tried, at least initially, to make the arrangement work. Carroll certainly was not threatened by George's presence; he was far too secure in who he was and what he represented in that church for him to resent or be concerned about the presence of another pastor.[10] George also was an experienced pastor and denominational leader who was not trying to usurp but rather to complement the roles and gifts of the other complex man. They seemed genuinely to like each other, at least at first, and genuinely to respect each other's very diverse abilities and interests.

However, those differences were surely part of the problem as well. The two men had different, even contrasting, personal and professional styles, which translated into different ways of thinking about and acting on leadership. Clashes started to occur, and congregants began to identify primarily with one or the other, especially as new people joined the church after George's arrival. The seamless garment began to unravel.

The arrangement probably would not have worked under any circumstances, for reasons noted above. No doubt the church did need time to let go of one pastor before embracing another; denominational wisdom is to be respected here. However, in this case there is another factor that has to do directly with issues of power and authority in the congregation: there was a cultural clash between the Presbyterian professionalism and procedural correctness that George introduced, and the rootedness of the social and political power of the kitchen cabinet that constituted another dynamic of power and authority with which George was not able to make peace. More specifically, George was neither comfortable with nor adept in the management of the more informal but also more longstanding power base upon which the clergy and lay authority of that church was exercised. He was never able to find a place at the kitchen table.

Carroll tried to include George in the process, formally uncharted but familiar to those at St. Matthew's. As we have seen, it was the practice for power and authority to operate on two levels at St. Matthew's, and for the most part they did so with grace and harmony. Several accounts of Carroll's leadership methods combined exasperation and affection as they told of the phone calls to raise the $20,000, or whatever the amount, to do whatever needed doing. Others spoke with the same tolerance, as though for family eccentricities, of the fact that important decisions got made outside the committee meetings and were rubber-stamped by the official groups. Samuelson was so deeply trusted on so many levels that even occasional discomfort with his authority was usually wrapped in affection and acceptance. At the same time, it was the case, as I outlined above, that virtually anyone with the time and energy to give could become active and even influential to a degree in the life of St. Matthew's church.

Those two levels broke apart at the time of the copastorate controversy. The seeds of the rupture were planted in the five years that the two pastors essentially split those two power bases. Although Carroll tried to include George in the discussions, telephone calls, and informal meetings that constituted his power base at St. Matthew's, George did not often choose to participate. That choice was partly a function of his personality and partly a function of commitment to a more open structure and more public procedures in running a church. Prior to George's arrival, there was no formal budget of any kind, there was virtually no structure in place for lay participation across a range of the church's life (though what structure there was was open), and there were no review processes for employees. The lack of formal structure is problematic for a church, at least one as large and affluent as St. Matthew's. Without such structure, the potential for abuses of all kinds is enormous. Furthermore, the programmatic implementation that George was able to bring about dramatically strengthened lay participation and leadership in the life of the church.

With this kind of authorized formal structure finally in place, the two kinds of power and authority, which had functioned together for so long with only occasional tension, lined up as open adversaries behind the two men. Carroll and George ended up representing the two opposing kinds of power, authority, and leadership; one a kind of aristocratic oligarchy, the other a more open, democratic approach.

The nastiness that surrounded the copastorate issue had never surfaced before in the history of the church. Even in the sixties, people left before they got ugly with one another. And yet, even through the painful memories, members of St. Matthew's point with pride to the fact that almost no one left the church over the conflict regarding the copastorate. Even those who had been most vocal, and most wounded, remained in the church. Had George decided to stay in the face of the narrow margin of support he had, the outcome could have been very different. His leaving may have been his final pastoral, healing gesture to the church he worked so hard to serve. The structures that he put in place at St. Matthew's still shape the church's life to a great extent, including the ways in which power and authority are understood and exercised.[11]

One final observation on this uncharacteristically emotional and hostile period in St. Matthew's history will help us not only to understand that time but to observe what changes will and will not be welcome as the leadership of St. Matthew's changes. Several people commented that the transition team that supported George Lewis's succession as senior pastor, over objections by most of the Session and others in the church, was naive about what would be involved in its job. They were also unequipped by the practices and expectations of the congregation to do what they were charged to do. The church relies on experts to maintain the smooth and professional running of the church, and in this case, there was a lacuna of expertise.[12] The pastors could not manage the situation because they were the issue. The church's self-image as a maverick included its scepticism regarding the expertise of its denominational leaders, even though the relations were much closer during George's tenure. Furthermore, the church failed to identify ahead of time the deep and multifaceted complexities of transition, particularly with the leadership constellation they had in place. St. Matthew's was and is not accustomed to handling things badly, and in this instance, they clearly did.[13]

Beginning to Heal

George left and returned to the New York area. Carroll resigned according to his original schedule. The highly competent members of St. Matthew's reclaimed the heritage of excellence and graciousness and intellectual rigor that had marked the church from the beginning. They gathered their considerable resources, both tangible and intangible, and began the business of moving on. They formed a search committee, brought in denominational expertise, and hired interim ministers. And the church entered the next phase of its life.

Some of those who had been most deeply embroiled in the controversy and pain of the process, and lack of process, of the previous two years withdrew from active participation in the church. However, as I said above, almost no one withdrew their membership. Both levels of power and authority were discernibly at work in the search process, and no apparent lasting damage had been done to the church. The episodes, painful though they were, provided a break with the past and reenergized commitment to a future that honored the past and yet moved in some new directions.

NOTES

1. As the founding pastor put it, when the church was built, the members characteristically decided to do it right, and they hired the best architect they could find. Their commitment to excellence in all aspects of their life is embodied in the very buildings that house that life.

2. When we began interviewing, we soon discovered that we weren't the first or the only ones to use that phrase!

3. Since the communion table is located at the back wall of the chancel it is not a functional part of worship, though it remains a visual center as it serves as a stand for the Roman cross and flowers.

4. I do not mean to imply by this account that the openness with which we now are beginning to confront clergy sexual abuse is anything but a tremendous advance for the churches, for individual persons, and for our society as a whole. What we are all coming to learn is that the general presumption of benevolence and innocence on the part of those in power has often been mistaken, and persons were damaged severely. It may be that the experience of the people at St. Matthew's and the benevolence and innocence of that group and its pastor were more the exception than the rule.

5. When someone suggested a guest registry for Sunday worship services, Samuelson dismissed the idea by saying, "Why would we do that? I know all the members." [Sally Purvis interview with anonymous source.]

6. Interview, March 1993.

7. That assessment may seem unduly harsh or dismissive. No doubt persons made contributions to the life of St. Matthew's that were helpful. Still, we recount the lived memories of the present and ex-members of St. Matthew's without any attempt to correct them from a perspective outside the church. More often than not,

Carroll Samuelson was the only clergyperson mentioned by church members before the events I am about to relate.

8. In spite of Carroll's unconcern with church growth, the church was growing, although it grew more rapidly after George joined the staff.

9. It struck us as uncharacteristic of St. Matthew's that the contract with George would have been so vague regarding this very important point.

10. We looked for evidence that he had been threatened, and we found none. There just did not seem to be any sort of turf wars going on, however likely that might seem now.

11. As was noted above, an outsider might view the outcome of the decision to move the school as more of a crisis than the copastorate issue, since in the former case almost half the members left and in the latter, almost no one left. That the former set of events is not considered to be a crisis in the church's history and the latter is unanimously proclaimed as the most difficult time the church endured is revealing of the values and self-identity of St. Matthew's.

12. Persons have said that the one person who might have provided such expertise in interpersonal and group dynamics and process had died the day before Carroll announced his retirement.

13. The church learned its lesson well. When there were some delicate personnel issues to address after Suzanne's arrival, the church asked a management consultant to do an analysis and submit a professional report with recommendations, which were later implemented, that proved enormously helpful. The outcome, and the process, would no doubt have been quite different if the matter had been addressed by an ad hoc group without the expertise of the professional consultant.

5   An Intergalactic Search

Moving Forward

Once the decision was made to conduct a national search for a senior minister, the committee was formed, and the process was undertaken with St. Matthew's characteristic commitment to excellence. Committee membership included persons from both sides of the copastorate issue, as well as some persons who had not been centrally involved. This time the process went by the book, with experts from the presbytery and the denomination, three interim pastors over the two-year search process, and consultations with many respected representatives of the denomination and the community.

The interim period went smoothly in part because the process was so carefully implemented and because it was so clearly interim. None of the three pastors was St. Matthew's type, especially "the minister from California" as he is indelibly known. Parishioners still shake their heads over his casual liturgical style, which they refer to as "laid back," and his innovative decision to change the color of the worship bulletins, an apparently radical step.[1] Yet he is spoken of with fondness, as are the other two interim ministers. It is fair to say, I think, that they officiated between ministers, and they themselves were never quite seen as the minister of St. Matthew's, a reality that is both the challenge and the health of interim ministry.

Having begun the search and being fully committed to its process, the committee mounted what they call "an intergalactic search" for the best minister St. Matthew's could find. Formally, at least, they were open to considering anyone, though the heritage and identity of excellence, intellectual rigor, theological flexibility, and the social homogeneity of the congregation set several informal limits to the range of candidates. Gender was not thought to be a significant factor, since it appeared that there were no qualified applicants who were female, although in principle the church was willing to examine such a person, if she in fact existed.

One of the persons who served as a consultant to the search committee was the Reverend Suzanne Jefferson. Suzanne was then the senior minister at a smaller Presbyterian church in an area that Atlantans think of as part of the city and its residents think of as a separate town. Prior to that appointment, she had been associate minister at one of the large downtown Presbyterian churches in Atlanta. She was nationally known and respected both for her preaching—she was called upon to lead preaching workshops around the country—and for her commitment to churches' involvement in social justice issues, especially issues related to homelessness. She was the impetus for the downtown church to begin a large on-site homeless shelter; when she moved to the second church, she was instrumental in its opening a homeless shelter for children. She was married to a prominent Atlanta lawyer, and she had been a visible member of several parts of the Atlanta community for some time. Since she was also active in Presbyterian circles, she was thought to be a valuable resource as the committee conducted its intergalactic search. She, in turn, was happy to be of help.

In the meantime, the church was healing and beginning to move on. After forty years with the same pastor, and after the uncharacteristic interactions that marked the copastorate issue, the time spent under the three interim ministers was an important respite. It also helped to sharpen the congregation's requirements for the person it would eventually call as its leader. Seventy-five percent of the members listed preaching as the most important skill for their senior pastor. Other qualities they were looking for included maintaining the tradition of excellence in all aspects of church life, preserving the church's commitment to community outreach, and honoring and nurturing its traditions of outstanding educational, artistic, and musical programs and offerings.[2] As one church member put it, they were looking for "someone bright, with intellectual integrity, someone 'more spiritual' than Samuelson had been, a good preacher, a good administrator, a warm, loving person who would go out into the community and spread good will."[3] In addition, the person would have to fit with the social profile of this church and respect its values, including its rejection of southern fundamentalism. Specifically, anyone who was uncomfortable with southern culture and who was intimidated by wealth and prestige could never lead this church.

These were not easy specifications, and although the members of St. Matthew's knew that their job opening was immensely appealing and likely to attract extremely talented candidates, they were approximately two years into the search and still had not found the right person. At that point the chair of the search committee called someone he knew at Princeton Seminary to ask who was the most outstanding up-and-coming pastor in the Presbyterian denomination. The man from Princeton replied, "Suzanne Jefferson."

The committee was intrigued by his response. In many ways she was a natural for the job, and they had gotten to know her and to like her as she worked with them as a consultant. However, there was a complication. It is not the usual practice for one church to call as their pastor someone who is currently serving a church in the same town, another piece of denominational wisdom that is usually worth following. However, after consultations with presbytery officials, it was decided that her proximity would not be an insurmountable obstacle to her call.

As the chair of the search committee gleefully announced to the congregation, "the best man for the job is a woman!" The intergalactic search unearthed a female minister serving in St. Matthew's side door. As one former church member put it, "Their choosing Suzanne was about as likely as God appearing in the body of a Jewish boy in first-century Palestine. I now believe in divine intervention!"[4]

The Best Man for the Job Is a Woman

In its own much more restrained style, St. Matthew's was as delighted with itself for calling a woman to the position of senior pastor as Bethany was tickled to call Cameron as its rector. A number of factors account for St. Matthew's decision. First, of course, was that Suzanne was the best man for the job. She, more than anyone, came with the constellation of qualities and abilities and gifts and experience that fit what looked like an impossible job description. In addition, she met the unwritten requirements with the possible exception of her gender. At the same time, St. Matthew's does pride itself on being a maverick church in relation to Southern Presbyterianism, even though the church had actually done nothing unusual for decades. Calling a woman was a way to reclaim a part of its treasured heritage.

The call of Suzanne Jefferson to St. Matthew's Presbyterian Church was very recent history when we began our research. For purposes of our study and for the issues this account raises regarding the understanding and exercise of power and authority in the two churches we studied, it is important to remember that we entered St. Matthew's at a point dramatically different from Bethany's relatively long-term relationship with its female leader. Cameron had been rector of Bethany for more than six years when we arrived, and Suzanne was at the beginning of her second year when our site research commenced. The different stages at which we viewed the women's ministries provided us with interesting contrasts, but we were very cautious about comparisons, especially in light of what we had observed of the growth in affection and trust between Cameron and her church over the years.

One of the first contrasts we encountered was the reluctance, or, more accurately, caution with which our research project was viewed by St. Matthew's. Suzanne had been there long enough for congregants to be delighted with their choice. She had, in the first year, proven to be everything they had thought she would be, and there was still a kind of excitement over the new relationship, rather like the early stages of a courtship. And like new lovers, both Suzanne and her church were very protective of one another. In particular, St. Matthew's did not view Suzanne's gender as a negative aspect of her ministry or her presence, and some members with whom we spoke were concerned that our research would create a problem where none existed. Once we assured them that we were not there to find problems and that we were really more interested in successes, we were welcomed with warmth and graciousness. The defensiveness we encountered, I believe, was directly attributable to the newness of the experience of Suzanne's pastorate for all involved.

In some respects the congregation of St. Matthew's was less prepared than Bethany's for female leadership. You will recall that the search committee of Bethany had prepared the congregation for that eventuality whereas initially St. Matthew's did not seem seriously to entertain the possibility that a female candidate would meet all their requirements. However, when their expectations were overturned, the congregation was very accepting, and their acceptance fits St. Matthew's pattern of trusting the leadership, clergy or lay, to do well the job they were given.[5] If the search committee decided that the best man for the job was a woman, then other persons in the church were ready to agree. The theme of Suzanne's general competence as the antidote to concerns regarding her gender played like background music in many of the interviews we conducted. One of the clerks of Session articulated the general feeling when he said, "People like having a woman minister with whom they can so fully identify and who is so flat-out good."[6] She fit and even reinforced St. Matthew's fundamental identity as maverick and excellent.

Navigating New Territory

The two different but congruent sources and styles of power and authority that were discussed in the previous chapter were very much in place when Suzanne arrived at St. Matthew's. Some of the personnel of Samuelson's kitchen cabinet had changed through the interim period, but an informal group composed of mostly well-to-do persons who are active and influential in powerful positions outside of St. Matthew's constitutes an important presence in the life of the church. The many persons active on the boards and ministries or committees of St. Matthew's are also active and important, especially after the structural reform instituted by George Lewis and continued and expanded since his departure. Both groups function very effectively and more or less in harmony.

The renovation of the manse provides an example of the combination at work after the decision to call Suzanne but prior to her actual arrival. The official structure of the church includes a property committee which theoretically had oversight of the renovation of the senior minister's home. The lovely old brick house is located adjacent to the church, and by all accounts it was badly in need of restoration. There was general consensus that such a project should be undertaken. There was much less formal agreement, however, on how extensive and expensive the project should be. As it turned out, the renovation of the manse cost as much as the value of the manse prior to renovation.

After the renovations were complete, a couple of people who had been on the property committee commented that they were unaware the project would be so extensive and costly, and they were able to identify the two people who made it happen. There was some concern on their part about the appropriateness of spending the money but apparently no anger or resentment about the informal way the process had been handled, even within a committee. The manse is beautiful and elegant, in keeping with the church itself. Suzanne uses the manse for church functions, and therefore parishioners are able to see it and enjoy it. The whole operation is a compact example of how things are done at St. Matthew's and of how the two levels of power and authority operate so well together.

Members of the congregation itself seldom use the word class, though to an outsider the social and economic homogeneity of the congregation is one of its prominent features. Several persons with whom we spoke were articulate about the comfort they feel with the homogeneity of the congregation and with the traditions of excellence in worship and education. (When St. Matthew's members speak about diversity in their church, they are almost always referring either to a spectrum of theological positions or to the intergenerational character of the congregation.) The setting, the people, and the activities constitute a unity that is comforting and somehow restful. This congruence is reinforced officially, when necessary, in some aspects of the church's life. For example, their policy of allowing only church members and their families to be married at the church is articulated in terms of upholding St. Matthew's standards for liturgy and especially music. It seems that during the interim period, some nonmembers held weddings that included soloists who "were not very good" and wedding liturgies that were not in accordance with St. Matthew's customs. Apart from the usual logistical concerns with scheduling and the availability of pastoral services, St. Matthew's uses the policy of restricting weddings to members in order to uphold its standards of excellence.

Without multiplying examples, these are some of the complex theological, social, and interpersonal waters that the new pastor had to navigate. Furthermore, the person who had been chair of the search committee that called Suzanne, the person who would ordinarily act as mentor and orientation guide, abruptly left the church for difficult personal reasons. It was an exciting, anxious, challenging, and often exhiliarating time for the church and for Suzanne Jefferson.

It was clear from the beginning, or at least by the second year when we began to observe the church, that Suzanne was comfortable with and adept at managing both kinds of power and authority that were so prominent at St. Matthew's. She ran a very smooth meeting, as did most of the committee chairs that we were able to observe. (In fact, a disorganized, inefficient meeting was a startling exception; in the year that we observed all kinds of meetings, we saw only one that was not well conducted.) In an official setting she was both charming and playful on the one hand, and businesslike and efficient on the other. She had done her homework on whatever issue was at hand, and she knew who in the group was in charge of what. If private lobbying were a necessary step in the process of meeting her goals, that lobbying had been completed before the meeting began.

In social settings, Suzanne's warmth and personal charisma were even more apparent. She combines southern charm and quickwittedness to create easy social exchanges. She moves around a room well and pays close attention to whomever she is speaking with at the moment. She is in every way at home in the social setting of St. Matthew's, and others feel at home as well in her presence.

On the interpersonal level, of course, we had much less chance to observe her at work, but reports of her pastoral skills suggest that she is also adept in that area. In fact, the tragic illness and death of the young adult daughter of one of the most prominent and beloved families of the church inaugurated Suzanne's deeply effective pastoral relationship with the congregation. She was accepted as pastor by the young woman, by the family, and by the church as she offered to all of them a deeply needed ministry of presence in that difficult time.

In summary, it seemed as though the intergalactic search had been worth every tiring meeting and phone call. St. Matthew's had found the perfect senior minister.

The Threat of the Gospel

In a symbolic and embodied dramatic upheaval, Cameron Clark turned around the sanctuary at Bethany Episcopal Church. Groundwork for the upheaval had been laid by the liturgical reforms of the Episcopal Church and, in another dimension, by the leadership lacuna that Cameron's forceful personality was called to fill.

At St. Matthew's, during the first summer of Suzanne's presence as senior minister, an anonymous gift was responsible for the unheralded appearance of pew Bibles in the sanctuary of St. Matthew's Presbyterian Church. It is possible that quiet gesture signaled an upheaval at St. Matthew's that will be every bit as dramatic as that which took place at Bethany.

There is, of course, nothing unusual about having pew Bibles in sanctuaries of mainline Protestant churches. In fact, it is unusual not to find them. And that, of course, is the point. St. Matthew's identity was shaped and sustained by its stance in opposition to Southern Presbyterianism as Samuelson and St. Matthew's parishioners interpreted it. I noted above that "bibliolatry" was one of Samuelson's favorite themes, and the whole constellation of associations surrounding Bible-belt Christianity is anathema to St. Matthew's.

Competent, energetic, socially sophisticated, politically astute, intellectually gifted, an outstanding preacher with a national reputation, committed to social justice, a warm and caring person—all these qualities made Suzanne Jefferson the perfect choice to lead St. Matthew's. However, Suzanne Jefferson is a Christian, openly and unapologetically. She is not a fundamentalist as St. Matthew's understands that term, but she is much more conventionally Christian than many of the long-term members of the church and certainly more so than Carroll Samuelson. Ironically, perhaps, that caused greater concern among persons with whom we spoke than any other issue. In order to illustrate the points of tension, if not conflict, between Suzanne's Christian convictions and the theological posture of many of the more long-term members, it will be helpful first to take note of the use, or lack of use, of theological language at St. Matthew's and second to discuss their different interpretations of the theological roots of ethical values.

When we first began observing worship and meetings and other events at St. Matthew's, we were struck by how little "God-talk" we heard. We certainly did not expect the language of fundamentalism and would have been shocked if, in that setting, anyone had asked us if we were saved. On the other hand, we did not expect that this extremely articulate congregation would apparently have so little language with which they could comfortably talk about spiritual realities. Nor would it have been possible to anticipate the remarkable distance between the self-definition of these people and the Christian story. The stories of the faith, whether from the Old Testament or the New, did not shape persons' accounts of their own lives or the life of their church in any significant way. It has been our experience that even very liberal Christian churches use the language of faith journeys, wrestling with God, confronting powers and principalities, and dealing with sin and evil. Not so at St. Matthew's to any noticeable degree.

On the other hand, Suzanne's language is peppered with allusions to biblical characters and stories. She has been shaped by them and both consciously and seemingly unconsciously continues to interpret her own experience through them. I do not mean that she engages in prooftexting or obvious biblical quotation, though she certainly can do so. Rather, biblical names and illustrations weave in and out of her speech in ways that suggest their ongoing hermeneutical function in her own life. Again, this is not unusual, even for liberal ministers. It is, however, a stark contrast to the language of St. Matthew's. Even when in interviews we occasionally asked persons very direct questions about their spiritual journeys or relationship with God, we more often than not encountered blank looks followed by inarticulate attempts to comply with our request. Certainly a few of the members of St. Matthew's are at home with Christian language and stories, but not many. In some important respects, at least at the beginning, Suzanne and her congregation were speaking in different tongues.

The other remarkable contrast is around the issue of the theological roots of ethical convictions. Over and over again we heard from parishioners that the impetus for their personal commitment to community service and outreach was guilt. Guilt was the word that the congregation used to characterize its own ethical motives. We heard many versions of the theme that of those to whom much had been given, much would be asked, though without the biblical echo. Persons were aware that their lives were advantaged in every way our society identifies, and there was a deep sense of obligation to share of the abundance.

Suzanne, on the other hand, preached more than once, even in the few months we attended worship services, of the joy of service and giving. In personal conversation, she is open about her own need to serve others and the sense of fulfillment and meaning that service brings her. The theology from the pulpit suggests that need and gratitude, not guilt, are the roots of concern for others. For Suzanne, shared vulnerability undergirds the obligation to reduce an inequitable distribution of goods, and shared vulnerability is at the heart of community outreach with the hands stretched in both directions. That is a difficult message for many members of St. Matthew's to hear.

The major challenge, then, that Suzanne Jefferson's ministry at St. Matthew's posed to the congregation, and to her, was related not to Suzanne's gender but to the contrast in styles of being Christian. Could the pew Bibles that had mysteriously appeared that first summer become not an oddity but an actual point of reference and source of a common language for this pastor and her church?

Building the Staff

No minister, however talented and energetic, could possibly provide an adequate pastoral presence for this church of approximately 1400 members. One of the church's initial tasks, then, after calling Suzanne, was to complete the professional clergy staff, a process in which Suzanne had an active role. The church hired as an associate pastor a young man who had been senior pastor of a small rural church and who was working on his Ph.D. in Old Testament at Vanderbilt. St. Matthew's faltering youth ministry was taken over by a married couple who were finishing their M.Div. degrees at the local Presbyterian seminary. Subsequent to two years' very successful part-time work in that capacity, they were called by

the church after their graduation. Another staff member was an ordained pastoral counselor who left his staff position, but continues
to do counseling on the premises under the auspices of a pastoral
counseling group with which the church has close ties.

The clergy staff seems to function well together, although the
size of the church and consequent division of responsibilities preclude the intimate, familylike relationships that obtain at Bethany.
The clergy offices, located on the second floor of one wing of the
main church building, are well appointed, and there are numerous
persons engaged in support activities. All are gracious, helpful, and
competent.

Many members of St. Matthew's Prebyterian Church refer to
their senior pastor as their CEO. There are a number of reasons for
that. First, many of the men in the church work in law offices and
businesses where the language of corporate American is a kind of
native tongue. Second, Suzanne's leadership style is forceful and
dynamic with an emphasis on efficiency, not unlike that of a CEO.
Third, the size of the church staff and the elegant appointments of
the office space create the feeling of a small, thriving business.
Meetings are held with the organizational skill and task orientation
of corporate American culture, and in many aspects of the church's
life, a corporate ethos predominates. CEO fits.

I noted that many men of the church came from corporate Atlanta, or were its lawyers. The profile of church members prior to
Suzanne's arrival included a division of gender roles that is fairly
traditional. Many of the wives of the lawyers and businessmen are
also community leaders in various capacities, but they are for the
most part volunteers. There were a few women with paid careers
and some single women who worked to support their families, but
the most visible group exercised traditional roles. As we were ending our site research, the profile was shifting a bit as church membership increased in response to Suzanne's presence and all that
her presence affected. Many of the new members were younger
people who reflected a somewhat greater diversity of social roles.
Nonetheless, the church has the look and feel of a social group that
is coupled along traditional lines.[7]

Suzanne, then, was CEO of a complex operation with a largely
corporate social profile—several staff members, over 1,400 members and growing, and extensive resources, both human and financial. The rather traditional, homogeneous, sophisticated, and
affluent membership continued to function within a self-image
whose centerpiece was a tradition and ongoing practice of excellence and intellectual openness, and the congregation continued to

define itself in contrast to southern Christian fundamentalism. All this presented the new senior minister with enormous challenge and enormous opportunity.

The Family House Shelter

In late fall of 1991, Suzanne got a phone call from the Atlanta Task Force on the Homeless, a group she had helped form and with whom she had worked for several years. The weather in Atlanta was turning cold, the established shelters were full to overflowing, and children were sleeping under desks in the Task Force office. A crisis was looming. Could Suzanne and her immensely resourceful church respond?

As usual, appeals to the needs of the homeless touched Suzanne, and she began conversations to assess the possibility of St. Matthew's itself housing a couple of homeless families. The church certainly had the space: large rooms and bathrooms with shower facilities on the bottom floor of one wing of the church building.

Suzanne's initial conversations with church members engendered a range of responses. Those responses and the shelter experiment that St. Matthew's undertook exposed to us layers of group interactions and the beginning of a shift in the ethos of St. Matthew's. We turn, then, to the chain of events and the responses they evoked in order to examine at a deeper level issues of power and authority in this congregation.

During our research into the understanding and practices of power and authority at Bethany Episcopal Church, we were able to see and understand a mutuality and interdependence between the leadership of the rector and that of the congregation that we had sensed but had not observed in any sustained way prior to the crisis of John's illness. What had appeared to us as a pattern of dominance and control was revealed to be a deeply relational, interactive dynamic in the leadership of the congregation. We then were able to take what we had learned about the church from the crisis we observed and reinterpret our previous observations with a more nuanced and complete narrative.

St. Matthew's experiment with the shelter provided us with a somewhat different opportunity. We had been able to observe and articulate the dual power structure of the church from histories and ongoing dynamics, and the dual power structure that I described above was in evidence during the shelter experiment. What we were able to observe, rather, was the emergence of a third constituency in addition to the remnants of the "kitchen cabinet" that continued to wield enormous power and influence and in addition to the more formal structure with its ministries and task forces that was charged with much of the actual operation of the church. This third constituency was composed mostly of new members, persons who had joined either after Suzanne's arrival at St. Matthew's or in the interim period just preceding her and who had not been so deeply shaped by the narrative tradition of the maverick church with its insistence on intellectual openness and excellence in everything it did. A number of persons in this third group were young, and while they were attracted to many of the same qualities of the church that had formed its identity in earlier years, they also brought more comfort with traditional Christian language, practices, and piety. They also had a different understanding of Christian service, one that was much closer to Suzanne's and that departed from the historical emphasis of the church.

Just as the identity of Bethany Episcopal Church is formed by the liturgical, eucharistic practice at its core, so the identity of St. Matthew's had been shaped by the narrative of its formation, its values of intelligence and excellence, its commitment to integration and social justice, and its emphasis on community outreach. What the founding narrative of the church meant by community outreach was active participation on the part of church members in the social and political affairs of the city. Several people told us that Carroll Samuelson was committed to the principle that the time and energy of St. Matthew's members was best spent in boardrooms and other influential decision-making bodies rather than in hands-on activities of community service. Furthermore, St. Matthew's community outreach included generous contributions on the part of the church and of individual members to those groups where the St. Matthew's presence could be felt. Christian service, then, was deeply integrated into the social, professional, and political activities of the members of St. Matthew's. Generosity with time and material resources was a posture that was nurtured in the founding narrative of the church and practiced out of a sense of privilege and power.

When the identity of a church is shaped around liturgical practice, then that church can accommodate multiple stories about who it is and was and will be, and it can even absorb conflicting accounts for a while. Diverse narratives are held together by a common liturgical core. When, on the other hand, the very identity of a church is largely constituted by a common story, a story whose boundaries function to shape the boundaries of the community, then the narrative can tolerate only limited flexibility, reinterpretation, and amendment before it and the church become something and someone else. The identity of St. Matthew's was dependent upon the narrative we have recounted many times and that was recounted for us with astonishing consistency by many persons in the church, both old-timers and newcomers. A dramatic departure from St. Matthew's way of doing things, then, not only triggered normal anxiety about change but threatened the very self-image of the group. The copastorate issue constituted such a departure, and it was unanimously cited as the crisis of the church.

In a far less dramatic fashion, the Family House Shelter experiment constituted a departure from the community service chapter of the narrative that was St. Matthew's. Though there was no overt, outright opposition to the shelter, neither of the established power bases—the kitchen cabinet or the Session—was fully behind the concept and for the most part did not participate in organizing or staffing the shelter. Furthermore, the organization and service focus of the project was very different from past practice. What this project enabled us to see, then, was the emergence of this third group with its somewhat different understandings of service and power and authority at what may have been a pivotal moment of change in the life of the church.

As I noted above, after the phone call from the Task Force on the Homeless, Suzanne had a number of conversations with various groups in the church. From all accounts, the clergy staff was unanimously in favor of at least exploring the feasibility of having an on-site shelter. By contrast, most of the older, more established church members were not. Their concerns were both logistical and philosophical.

The logistical concerns were shared by nearly everyone, although there was a range of opinions regarding their seriousness. The geographical location of St. Matthew's, in the wealthy, northwest area of Atlanta a long bus ride from downtown, rendered it an unlikely location for a homeless shelter. Since it would operate only from six at night until seven in the morning, the guests would have to find somewhere else to stay during the day, and that would mean getting transportation to another area of the city where the day shelters were. St. Matthew's was, indeed, an odd location for a homeless shelter.

The more serious objections, however, had to do with whether an on-site shelter was the best use of St. Matthew's resources. Under the established concept of community service, it was much more effective for St. Matthew's members to continue to work with the city of Atlanta to alleviate the causes of homelessness, to

provide job training and other services, and to establish larger public facilities for those who remained homeless. The church could
accommodate only two families at a time, and the entire project
would be staffed with volunteers from St. Matthew's. It was enormously cost ineffective in terms of human resources.

These concerns and others regarding security, screening of residents, and organization of volunteers were widely shared. Two
groups of younger adults in the church, however, articulated another perspective on the project and were responsible for its adop-
tion, its organization, and its staffing. The two groups—one mostly
in their twenties, the other mostly in their thirties—were organized
both for social and service activities. Several persons who were active in the shelter project expressed variations of a common concern that while St. Matthew's had a strong tradition of community
service, that service meant writing checks and sitting on boards.
The members of these younger groups wanted more hands-on service. Several of them volunteered in other shelters in town, and
they were eager for their own church actually to be a place of service to others.

From the beginning, the shelter project helped to focus these
two understandings of community service, and there was a thinly
disguised negative assessment by each group of the approach of
the other. Persons were always polite, of course, in their descriptions, but the gulf was apparent. And at least in part the fundamental question was, What is the nature of the church?, which in
turn related to the self-understanding of the people who were the
church of St. Matthew's.

The less than enthusiastic response by the informal power
structure was countered by the enthusiasm of the younger groups.
With the acquiescence of the Session, a study group was formed,
and two or three persons set about working with the appropriate
city agencies to find families who were homeless but who would
soon qualify for their own housing. At the same time, the structure
of the project itself was outlined and various persons were recruited
to find persons to staff the project at different times.

Working with the city agencies proved to be a frustrating experience, especially since the man who had assumed primary responsibility for doing so had a full-time job that required him to
travel. Locating the equipment that would be necessary to house
two families was a time-consuming but less frustrating job. As a result of these efforts, a report was made to the Session regarding the
feasibility of the Family House Shelter, and the Session approved
the project for an experimental three-month period. When a sign-

up sheet was passed around at the Session meeting asking people to volunteer either by bringing food or spending the night in the shelter, no one on the Session volunteered, much to the dismay of the young adults who were in charge of the project.[8]

Nonetheless, the Family House Shelter was launched with two families in residence and initial enthusiasm on the part of those involved. During the course of the three months, the usual mishaps and embarrassments one might expect in such a situation occurred, and some of the people from St. Matthew's who volunteered to serve in the project found interactions with the residents more difficult than they had anticipated. One family ended up leaving because the location was too difficult; another was asked to leave after a series of difficulties; and one family stayed nearly the whole time and moved into an apartment at the end of the three months.[9]

Assessment of the project is equivocal and depends upon who is asked and what is asked. Many people who were involved found it a rewarding and important experience. Almost everyone says that they learned a great deal about running an on-site shelter and could make very helpful organizational changes were it to be tried again. Most of the people who were most active felt overloaded at least once in the three months, although that did not diminish enthusiasm in every case.

It is certain that the project never received the support of the church as a whole, either conceptually or in terms of participation. In view of that fact, it is significant that such a departure from the common practice of St. Matthew's was able to happen at all. Without the wholehearted endorsement either of the kitchen cabinet or of the Session, enormous amounts of time and energy and some money went into the project. The groups of younger members that organized and ran the shelter were both exhausted and energized by the experience. Power and authority were spread and shared in new ways in this episode in a new kind of outreach to the community. That experience more than the project itself may be the triumph and important legacy of the Family House Shelter.

Conclusion

In many ways St. Matthew's choice to call Suzanne Jefferson as its senior pastor was in character, and the fact that she was a woman fit well with this church's self-image as a maverick. She brought to the job all of the qualities of leadership and social skills that the position required, and her personal charisma, intelligence, and long history in Atlanta only enhanced the good fit. She was willing to accept the challenge of leading this complex and immensely talented church, and they trusted that she would be the excellent leader they needed and wanted.

It is impossible to draw long-range conclusions or make confident predictions about the future of St. Matthew's under Suzanne's leadership. Predictions are impossible in any case, and our time with this church was very early in her stay there. What we can report is that the tensions that surfaced and the shifts in understandings and practices of power and authority that we did observe clustered around the energy of new groups of people whose concept of Christian service was in harmony with Suzanne's and a dramatic departure from St. Matthew's past. From Bibles quietly placed in the pews one summer day to the articulation of persons' need to serve in a hands-on way those who are in need, a shift was under way. A new chapter was being added to the narrative at the heart of St. Matthew's identity, with new characters, new plot, and new directions.

George Lewis told me that when he heard the church had called Suzanne Jefferson as senior pastor, he laughed and said, "At last, St. Matthew's is going to have biblical sermons on a regular basis," and he noted by her sermon titles that in fact that is the case. Suzanne's native language is biblical and rather traditionally Christian, and at least some members of St. Matthew's now share that language with her and interpret it much as she does. It would be wonderful to have a crystal ball to see whether, and how, the Christian narrative and the narrative of St. Matthew's can be reconciled.

One final note: The shelter experiment was not repeated the following year as a project for the church.

NOTES

1. A more radical step, which the congregation tolerated but did not embrace, was his insistence on the use of inclusive language in all aspects of the church's life, including worship. He was dismayed to learn that the practice ended when he left and that Suzanne does not necessarily use inclusive language in worship settings.
2. One area they were not interested in was church growth, and the issue of growth itself was, and continues to be, potentially divisive. I will return to this issue below.
3. Maggie Kulyk interview with a parishioner, undated.
4. Maggie Kulyk interview with parishioner, 17 September 1992.
5. Again, our project included dynamics of gender and role authority in consonance with the sociological research findings of Cathryn Johnson, cited in chapter 2.
6. Maggie Kulyk interview with a parishioner, 13 October 1992.
7. One person speculated that the fact Suzanne was married to a suc-

cessful Atlanta lawyer and had raised two children was important to her presence at St. Matthew's.

8. Accounts differ, actually, as to whether no one on the Session signed up or one or two did. However, the person who circulated the sign-up sheet told us he did not get one name that night.

9. I am purposely keeping this account vague in order to protect the privacy of the shelter guests.

6   Daughters of Jerusalem

The Changers and the Changed[1]

By all accounts and by virtually every measure, Cameron Clark and Suzanne Jefferson are supremely successful people. Not only are they leaders of their churches and occupants of outstanding vocational roles for persons of either gender, they are also by and large happy with their lives. Suzanne is happily married; Cameron is happily single. Both are struggling with issues and decisions regarding elderly parents, but those struggles locate them generationally with many of their parishioners, and both Suzanne and Cameron accept the struggles as a painful part of the passage of middle age. Both love their work and their churches.

We have seen some of the ways in which both women navigate the complexities of power and authority as those manifest themselves in their churches. In many ways they encounter and interact with different issues and challenges because of the denominational and social differences between their congregations. At Bethany, the interplay of hierarchy and egalitarianism, and the dynamic and sometimes subtle interdependencies of forceful, directive priest and powerful lay participation form the network of the negotiations of power and authority in the church. The liturgical center of the church's life and the relatively stable institutional loci for leadership combine in a way that encourage and accommodate a lively diversity of membership. Gender roles are relatively fluid, and tradition and innovation are at home with one another. In all these arenas and interactions, Cameron is present and the guiding force of much of the church's life.

At St. Matthew's, with its larger congregation and more homogeneous membership, Suzanne participates with agility and expertise in both the formal and informal power structures she inherited. Both groups confer authority upon her, and her abundant talent and excellent leadership reinforce it. More traditional Christian language and a more traditional Christian hermeneutic of everyday experience were prominent parts of Suzanne's presence as senior pastor of this church in the months we observed it. She skillfully negotiated and participated in the structures of power and authority even as she began to challenge some aspects of St. Matthew's identity during our on-site research. Nonetheless, her leadership—both her power and authority—was unquestioned, and her ability to lead the church, and persons' trust in her to do so, were clear.

While the situations and the challenges they face are different, there is no doubt that Cameron Clark and Suzanne Jefferson are outstanding clergy representatives of their denomination. They have both carried on and modified structures of power and authority that were in place in their churches. Their gender has not proved to be an impediment to their own success or to their facility in accomplishing the inordinately complex set of tasks that their jobs and their calling require. To recount the words of one member of St. Matthew's, they are women and they are "flat out good."[2]

And yet . . . precisely because of their outstanding success, Cameron and Suzanne both lead transgressive lives in the most conventional settings available in our culture. They opulently fulfill vocational expectations; they remain firmly and happily heterosexual females, "womanly women." They negotiate the power struggles in their congregation largely though not entirely successfully; their leadership styles cannot be characterized along the lines of gender expectations, either as male or female. In some important ways, they live as exceptions, and yet what they exceptionally are is conventional. They transgress neither vocational roles nor gender; they fulfill both. The combination is transgressive.

Much contemporary feminist theory and gay and lesbian theory focus on difference as a way to locate identity that is not defined by stable, patriarchal constructs but that hovers in some form or other at the edges or margins of those constructs. Moving far beyond Simone de Beauvoir's characterization of woman as "Other"[3] (though dependent upon her insights in often unacknowledged ways), a legion of postmodern/deconstructionist theorizing attempts to track an acknowledged but illusive realm beyond the logic of technological control that characterizes Enlightenment and post-Enlightenment concepts.[4] The postmodern decentering of human subjectivity is in part an articulation of the complexity and flux that characterize our time. Identity is shifting, being redefined, asserted, defended, and deconstructed. Value systems differ in significant and irreconcilable ways. Absolutes have receded and are receding.

Feminist theory has contributed to and celebrates the destabilization of the hegemony of white male privilege, however individual feminist theorists respond to various forms of postmodern proposals. Persons and groups who do not benefit from discursive and political arrangements are those who have the best critical perspective on them. Likewise, the creative and destabilizing work in gay and lesbian theory moves from perspectives that are disprivileged by constructs of sexual and gendered "normalcy." Normalcy itself becomes other and difference is privileged, albeit provisionally and within limits.

This study of two churches led by women, and observation of the women in their successful though not stereotypical professional lives, suggests the possibility of a different pattern of transgression than either the postmodern feminists or the gay and lesbian theorists propose. Cameron and Suzanne live their lives within conventional social constructs of gender and ministerial vocation. They are feminine females, and they are strong church leaders. And it is precisely this combination of conformities that constitutes the potentially transgressive aspects of their lives.

Using a linguistic metaphor, to some extent Cameron and Suzanne live their lives in incommensurate discourses. The discourse of feminine female is supposed to be incommensurate with, if not oppositional to, strong organizational and political leadership abilities. These women live them both. Thus they challenge the patriarchal, restrictive discourse of the social constructs of their reality not by transgendered activity, by unequivocal rejection of female roles, or by unconventional life forms. Rather they embody quite well roles our social scripts say cannot be played by one person and roles that involve socialization processes that may be contradictory.

bell hooks's 1984 book, *Feminist Theory: From Margin to Center*,[5] helped to popularize "marginality" as a term to express the social location of various oppressed groups. She, of course, was speaking primarily of African-American women, but the term has easy applicablility to any group in a position of relative powerlessness. Many groups who find themselves in marginal political or social positions have no choice but to transgress social norms of the powerful groups; race and sexual orientation are two demarcations of marginality. It is often the case that marginalized groups form alternative communities, complex and shifting though those communal groups may be.[6] Membership in those communities, then, may provide a center for persons at the margins.

hooks's work stands as another contrast to what we observed.

Cameron and Suzanne remain firmly within the boundaries of the center in virtually every aspect of their lives, private and professional. Their transgression, by contrast to membership in marginal groups, is their multiple membership in conventional groups that crosses and combines them in unconventional ways.

All transgressive behavior carries with it a cost. In the case of the pastors and the congregations we studied, the cost was only initially and provisionally born by the congregations. There was some risk associated with each church's decision to call a woman to lead it. As we noted, both churches' recent histories had prepared them in some ways for being different. In the case of St. Matthew's, the decision to call a woman reinforced their image as maverick and helped them to reclaim a prideful heritage after a painful and foreign time of wounding. In Bethany's case, their readiness for a strong leader and their already somewhat eclectic congregation created priorities that allowed for their ready acceptance of Cameron's dynamic and energetic presence.

However, it was quickly clear to both churches that their choices had brought them strong, trustworthy, and capable leaders. Both churches enjoyed, in their different ways, the exceptions that they became with their senior pastors, but the demands and challenges of their ongoing congregational lives soon eclipsed the issue of their pastor's gender. My research associates and I were skeptical of those who told us at the beginning of our research project that the pastor's gender isn't an issue. In a sense, they were right; the gender of the senior ministers did not compromise the administration of the church or care of its members.

For the pastors, however, the juxtaposition of their gender and their professional success has to remain an issue. Their transgressive embodiment of the incommensurate discourses that their lives enact constitutes an ongoing and often unexpected source of confrontation, suspicion, challenge, and isolation. Every new group, every new denominational executive, and every new crisis opens the possibility that they must defend the constellation of qualities and abilities and commitments that constitute their daily lives.

Both women encounter the dissonance of their own personalities, training, gifts, and choices. Sometimes the source is tied more to gender in instances when persons expect them to be more nurturing in some particular exchange because they are women. (Both women are very nurturing in a wide variety of settings.) Sometimes the source is tied more to profession in instances when their vulnerability is unexpected and rejected. (The latter is more rare than the former, though both women have experienced both.)[7] There is an instability in their occupation of the role of successful woman based upon the incommensurability of those terms in some versions of the gendering of our social settings, as well as in the women's ability to embody, and enjoy, a combination of roles that is supposedly inappropriate.

The transgressive juxtaposition of feminine women and social and political power is not, of course, confined to the two pastors of our study. Edward Lehman, Jr.'s, research into laypersons' reactions to women in ministry in several denominations in England and the United States shows that even strong resistence to a "lady" pastor or priest is most effectively overcome when persons are actually in contact with a female pastoral leader.[8] Other research, both formal and more anecdotal, uncovers the same pattern.[9] St. Matthew's Presbyterian Church and Bethany Episcopal Church expressed only limited resistance to calling a female senior pastor, and the resistance was outweighed by their conviction that the best man for the job was a woman and that the congregations themselves would be ready for the changes in experience and expectations of gender that their decision would eventuate.

The tension of living in the interstices of incommensurate discourses and incommensurate social roles that are of themselves conventional but transgressive in their combination is, I believe, a widely documented but relatively unexplored experience. Deconstruction of sexuality, gender, and embodiment expose ways in which dominant discourses construct the possibilities for human life in any society, but they also suggest the ways in which those discourses structure even the options for rebellion and nonconformity.[10] As Susan Bordo writes,

> The pleasure and power of "difference," I would once again insist against postmodern theorists, is hard-won; it does not bloom freely, insistently nudging its way through the cracks of dominant forms. Sexism, heterosexism, racism, ageism, while they do not determine human values and choices, while they do not deprive us of agency, remain strongly normalizing within our culture.[11]

Conventional embodiment of unconventional combinations of social expectations is transgressive, and as with more obviously unconventional displacements, there is a cost.

Along with the personal cost borne by the women, there is the ongoing effect of destabilizing gender expectations. It is impossible to know at this juncture of our history the degree to which the destabilization of gender expectations can be tolerated, and thus it is impossible to know the degree to which it will occur. Concurrently, it is difficult to predict the degree to which the personal costs borne by the pastors in our study will diminish the insults, isolation, and resentments for others who follow them into the same or similar transgressive combinations of conventional roles and behaviors.

The power and uncertainty of the transitional phase that we observed and documented is illuminated by the biblical story that functioned as an interpretive lens for this analysis. In Luke's gospel, after the crowds had chosen to release Barabbas and crucify Jesus, the passion story continues:

> As they led him away, they seized a man, Simon of Cyrene, who was coming from the country, and they laid the cross on him, and made him carry it behind Jesus. A great number of the people followed him, and among them were women who were beating their breasts and wailing for him. But Jesus turned to them and said, "Daughters of Jerusalem, do not weep for me, but weep for yourselves and for your children. For the days are surely coming when they will say, 'Blessed are the barren, and the wombs that never bore, and the breasts that never nursed.' Then they will begin to say to the mountains, 'Fall on us'; and to the hills, 'Cover us.' For if they do this when the wood is green, what will happen when it is dry?" (Luke 23:26–31, NRSV)

This pericope is poised at the moment of change—for the gospel writer—cosmic change. The end was unknown to the participants in the story; even the author of the gospel could not have anticipated the historical irresolution of the drama that he was recounting, and thereby to some extent constructing. The women were conscious of the pain of Jesus, present and impending, and were mourning as women do. Jesus, however, understanding the apocalyptic setting of this time, and the construct-bending, world-changing nature of his being, turned to them and challenged them away from the ordinariness of their weeping for others and toward the danger of their own lives.

With a loose and allusive reading of this text, it focuses for me my observations of a world poised on the edge of cataclysmic change with the danger and promise, the inevitability and uncertainty the moment evokes. It also focuses for me the unselfconscious weeping of the women for another and the challenge to Jesus to look to their own lives and the potential disaster in which they will be embroiled. Finally, it focuses for me the ambiguity of counterposing apocalytic and historical claims and hopes, utopic visions and the minutiae of ordinary lives.

There is in this pericope a haunting blend of despair and hope—despair in Jesus' lament for the present and future condition of the daughters of Jerusalem and hope woven into the apocalyptic context of this speech. In Jesus' story, crucifixion is resolved in resurrection. That sequence is at least a tantalizing possibility for the fate of the women themselves. It is also possible, of course, that there will be no redemption, no justice for the daughters of Jerusalem. When the wood is dry, the violence might be all-consuming. Nonetheless, there is the shadow if not the substance of hope. The other-directed nature of the women's lives and work, Jesus' call to the women to notice their own pain and the precariousness of their present and future situations, and the blending of hard reasons for despair with shadows of hope are all themes that emerged from this study.

I am interpreting our observations of two women's leadership of large, prestigious churches as a transgressive juxtaposition of social roles such that gender and role expectations are loosened and perhaps dislodged. I am arguing that the combination of conventional roles in unconventional ways helps to regender those roles and widen the range of possible social constructs for the process of gendering itself. Furthermore, the blending of gendered expectations in the lives of these feminine and forceful women provides some data for the counter-essentialist conclusion that women's ways of acting and being can encompass a wide, unstable, kaleidoscopic range of options and so help to deconstruct narrower interpretations and patterns of gendering. Our study suggests that it is not just those who are blatantly unconventional who challenge conventions; rather those who embody conventional roles in unconventional combinations contribute to the breakdown of traditional gender expectations and aid in the reinscription of the gendering of roles and persons.

It could be argued that there is no social transgression involved in the ability of some middle-class white women to embody roles that have traditionally belonged to middle-class white men. It could be argued that what we observed in the two churches led by women was the same old patriarchal exercise of power and authority transferred to the hands of a few "good girls" who maintain the status quo and subvert radical change. It could be argued that what we observed was a pernicious liberalism that colludes with business-as-usual and acts in opposition to social change for the truly oppressed.

It is the case that the shifts and unsettlings of traditional understandings of power and gender that we observed are subtle and elusive. We did, however, observe shifts and unsettlings, and the case study material we presented documents them. The refusal of these women and their churches to be contained by any stereotypical designations, the ongoing fluidity of the category of gender itself, the remarkable and dynamic generative interactions of the persons we observed, all suggest that the presence of female leadership in these churches is indeed part of a profound change in the roles of women and men and thus in the social construction of gender itself. We observed, interviewed, and consulted with two remarkable women, but as we have shown, their achievements are in part due to the often less visible achievements of women who preceded them. The two pastors, in turn, will have a part in preparing the ground for those who follow, both female and male.

More radical, overtly transgressive, politically self-conscious alternative social arrangements are important and necessary. I am not arguing that the quietly conventional, polite shifts that we observed and documented are the only effective vehicle for social change. They are, however, part of this era of transition, participating in the loosening of old roles and expectations and in the ongoing articulation of new ones. As the Lukan pericope suggests, the outcome is still uncertain.

Let us turn now to the churches themselves and articulate our observations regarding contested areas in their discourses of power and authority.

Bethany Episcopal Church

As we saw in chapter 3, Bethany Episcopal Church is able to incorporate the disparate elements of female priest with grace, humor, and delight. Cameron has been the rector long enough and has interacted with the church in such a wide variety of contexts that there are few surprises on either side of the altar regarding the regendering of the role of priest. Again, as was noted in chapter 3, members of the church cheerfully claim that they have a "mother," and Cameron's strong leadership style filled a need that was clear, compelling, and urgent. With the arrival of Lisa as assistant to the rector, and with the ongoing richness and success of Cameron's role as rector, changing expectations regarding gender and professional roles were familiar.

The tensions, however, were not absent. Some congregants expressed concerns regarding Cameron's forceful leadership style: occasionally it engendered appreciation and resentment at the same time in the same people. Furthermore, Cameron encountered the occasional sceptical visitor, and while she was widely respected by her (mostly male) denominational colleagues, her gender remained the occasional target of sexist attitudes and expectations. Battles won in one place tended to reconvene elsewhere.

What the focus issue exposed was the degree to which these tensions, and the understandings and practices of power and authority at work at Bethany, were cushioned by the inclusive and egalitarian strands in the life of the congregation. The centrality of the eucharistic liturgy, the widespread respect for social/psychological wisdom, and the partnership of power and authority among persons whose professions themselves waver at the edges of gender stereotypes were all factors in the dynamic openness and liveliness of this church. However, the interactions were far too complex to allow us to assign any relations of cause and effect. The focus issue may also have exposed some internalization of gender role rigidity in myself and my research assistant, even though our commitments and training are feminist, and we are not conscious participants in constructions of gender that guarantee the narrowing of women's lives. It may be that we had difficulty focusing on the way in which Cameron's assertive and forceful leadership style is consonant with a participatory, egalitarian partnership of power.

In any event, what we came to know is that leadership is directive at Bethany, but power is largely generative. What initially appeared as a pattern of power as control gave way to a much more nuanced picture of carefully delineated authority and widely shared power that was synergistic and life-giving.

As a kind of summary of the patterns of change and the conventionally transgressive nature of the regendering of roles at Bethany, recall the overlapping stories of Julia and Cameron. Julia's early options were circumscribed by her traditional choice to relinquish her responsibilities as a deaconess in Canada and to follow her husband in the role of rector's wife and church volunteer. The effective leadership that Julia provided to the church even in the limited bounds of authority available to her, and the respect and affection she evoked, were part of the background of female leadership as it had unfolded in the history of Bethany Church. In some sense, Julia's power in the church, unofficial though it may have been, and the power of other laywomen, helped to make possible Bethany's decision to call Cameron; Cameron is very open about the extent to which Julia has been pastor to the church and to Cameron. And Cameron, then, was influential in Julia's decision to be received as a deacon in the Episcopal Church, through encouragement and also surely by example, as Cameron enacted Woman and Priest so well. Their two stories move like narrative dancers on a shifting floor of possibilities and social worlds.

St. Matthew's Presbyterian Church

Suzanne and Cameron share the enactment of transgressive gender expectations discussed in this chapter, and the two women share the general characterization of successful, talented, loved, and respected senior pastors. But the situation at St. Matthew's with regard to the patterns and promises of change we have been developing is more complicated than that at Bethany.

The complications are many. First, our research there took place at a different point in the process of the development and embodiment of female power in the life of the church. You will recall that Suzanne was beginning her second year when we began our field research. There is an inevitable period of adjustment when any new pastor leads any congregation; this pastor's gender was just one among many facets of the relationship that was still being assessed.

Second, the wider social context of St. Matthew's includes more carefully delineated gender roles than does Bethany's. While Suzanne navigates the juxtaposition between being female and being professionally successful as gracefully as Cameron does, the effects of that conventional transgression are still to be measured. Transgression is a relational, contextual possibility. That is, the conventions of the social setting in which behavior and attitudes are enacted shape at least to some degree what counts as transgressive. Furthermore, contexts also enfold what can be imagined; transgression is in relation to some conventional claims, norms, and sanctions.

The social conventions of St. Matthew's are complex, largely inarticulated, and enforced. As we saw in chapter 4 and in even more detail in chapter 5, there is an understanding of what is and is not done at St. Matthew's. That understanding can be reformed, as in the case of Suzanne's insistence that staff salary increases be included in the annual meeting, even over objections that public discussions of salaries and income was "tacky." Nonetheless, the social mores, including pockets of very traditional understandings of gender roles, work within a narrower range at St. Matthew's than they do at Bethany.

Within that context, it is unlikely that Suzanne's generational contemporaries will envision choices for themselves that depart significantly from those they have already chosen. On the other hand, Suzanne's impact on a younger generation of northwest Atlanta could be deep and complex, as her example acts in concert with other professional women those young people are likely to encounter. The social world of St. Matthew's is changing slowly, but it is changing. While having a female senior pastor is in keeping with the maverick character of the church, the transgressive possibilities that Suzanne's leadership invokes comprise a new element and provide unforeseen potential for change.

In addition to Suzanne's shorter tenure and the more clearly defined social roles of her congregation, there is the added complexity of the dissonance, if not incommensurability, of the historical narrative of St. Matthew's church on the one hand and the biblical and historical narrative of Christianity on the other. The most profound and potentially unsettling change for St. Matthew's under the leadership of Suzanne Jefferson is the challenge that I outlined in chapter 5 regarding the "Threat of the gospel." The focus issue illustrated a shift by some members of the congregation, many of them the younger members, from what might be called benevolence at a distance to a more participatory involvement with persons who are less privileged. As we saw, the founding pastor of the church espoused a kind of cost-benefit argument when he encouraged persons to give material resources to charities but to use their time and energy and significant influence to reform conditions in the city as a whole. For Suzanne, and for those who were advocates of the Family House Shelter project, the Christian message includes activities that promote solidarity across race and class lines such that benevolence at a distance is envisioned as a disservice to the giver. There is, of course, no fundamental contradiction between close and personal involvement with persons across a range of social locations and political and economic reform. One could argue that the two are most effectively symbiotic. As the discussion was shaped at St. Matthew's, however, at least in the case of the shelter, the two approaches were articulated by two mostly different groups of people whose understandings of what was appropriate for St. Matthew's had been shaped by two theological interpretations. There was some conflict, then, at just the point of the interpretation of Christian mission, and that conflict represents and illustrates the potential conflict between narratives that shape the self-interpretation and ongoing life of St. Matthew's.

The fact that Suzanne is a female, the unconventional, off-center fact of her gender, enables her to function at St. Matthew's as a more traditionally Christian minister than St. Matthew's might otherwise embrace. Suzanne Jefferson is far from being a fundamentalist Christian as that appellation is understood by members of St. Matthews. However, in the particular history of this church, rejection of fundamentalism included almost wholesale rejection of traditional Christian language, and in that context, even Suzanne's sophisticated and nuanced use of the Christian narrative can be seen as a shift.

The quasi-reactive "not that" element of the core identity of the church required that their choice of a senior pastor be nontraditional. Suzanne's gender fulfills that requirement; her much more traditional Christianity is given space by her untraditional gen-der/role mix. To reiterate the claim of chapter 5, the deep shifts that our research began to detect are traceable to the clash of narratives. That clash, in turn, is made possible in part because Suzanne's gen-der enacts a central element in the old narrative at St. Matthew's, even as her theological convictions challenge that narrative.

Finally we need to consider the issue of the two styles of lay leadership that constituted the two power bases of St. Matthew's: the informal kitchen cabinet and the more formal structure of lay leadership at St. Matthew's. We traced their histories in chapter 4 and saw them at work in chapter 5. For most of the life of the church, the two groups and the two styles of power and authority coexisted without conflict, at least not overt conflict. The power and prestige of church members comes through the door of the church, and as we saw, Rev. Samuelson's impatience with the labyrinthine processes of ordinary church structure, as well as the deep and abiding trust between him and the church members, provided the perfect context for the more ad hoc assignment and exercise of lay leadership. Members of St. Matthew's are by and large immensely talented persons. They expect that persons who are given responsibilities will carry them out efficiently, and the cul-ture requires minimal checks and backup procedures for the exe-cution of leadership roles.

For the period of our on-site research, at least, Suzanne seemed comfortable with and accepting of both kinds of power. She was an agile, adept student of and participant in the formal, Presbyter-ian political process. She expanded the range and degree of lay par-ticipation even in the time we were there, and she did so largely by enhancing the structures in place and enlarging them and streamlining them when necessary. All of this was done with ap-parent ease and comfort on her part, and even the changes she adopted engendered only mininal concern. At the same time, Suzanne was sufficiently at home in the social and economic cul-ture that characterizes St. Matthew's so that she was neither threat-ened nor intimidated by the wealth and influence of the kitchen cabinet. As we saw, the informal decision-making process was clearly in place with regard to the renovation of the manse; she worked well with the key people in other settings as well.

The different power bases, then, among the laity at St. Matthew's, constitute a complexity, not a conflict. As it has in its past, so now the church seems comfortable encompassing a num-ber of channels of authority that intersect sources and kinds of power from inside and outside the church. It may be that over time and as church membership grows, and with normal attrition of older, influential church members, the kitchen cabinet will fade into history; but in any case, it is not likely to be a major source of strife. Both formal and informal authority at St. Matthew's seem flexible and resilient in the face of other changes the church is undergoing.

Conclusion

Our study of power and authority in two churches led by women, and the feminist analysis that we brought to the study, caught a moment in an era of tremendous social change. It is, of course, a moment that will be reenacted in somewhat other forms in other settings and other times; social change is an uneven process. Our study does not enable us to make sweeping, confident generalizations regarding gender except to demonstrate that gender itself is a fluid concept and part of the deep change at work in the social worlds that we observed. Even our two churches, similar as they are in many ways, provide contrasting examples of the roles of gender, the expectations around gender, and the rate and kind of change those expectations are undergoing.

At Bethany Episcopal Church, Cameron Clark has built and continues to build on seeds of inclusivity and gender equality that were there when she arrived, and she and her congregation have worked to expand the diversity of their membership regarding race and sexual orientation. The interaction between priest and laity, and among lay members of the church, is a complex combination of the special authority of the priest, embodied here by a woman, and the egalitarian, relational partnership that characterizes so much of the church's life. Cameron is the source of much of the vision and the energy of the church, and her leadership is undisputed. She also encourages and longs for and sometimes has thrust upon her, a shared responsibility with the laity for the well-being of the church.

Suzanne Jefferson's profile fits well at St. Matthew's. Her social location, her national reputation, and her sheer talent are at home there, and her gender contributes to the church's ongoing identity as maverick, exceptional, and progressive. Furthermore, her gender allows her to move toward, and move the church toward, a more traditionally Christian narrative, and perhaps a concomitant shift in how the church understands its relationship with those from vastly different social locations. As the focus issue illustrated, it is too soon to tell how the change will take place and the forms the change will take, but we have seen its inception.

Finally, this study has shaped the argument that the embodiment by these female pastors of traditional roles in combinations that are untraditional is transgressive and expansive of gender expectations. These women, and their churches, are part of a quiet revolution. They are not espousing or practicing radical social change; many of the church members and their clergy would probably work very hard to prevent radical social change in many of its forms. On the other hand, self-consciously or not, these groups and the women who lead them are not simply reinscribing patriarachal power and control. The transgressive combination of traditional roles here is a subtle and effective agent of change. The ability of Cameron Clark and Suzanne Jefferson to live in the midst of incommensurate discourses and to continue to function so effectively in all of them, holds forth the promise of new discourses, even with some of the same old vocabulary. There is also the possibility that new words will emerge.[12]

Like the daughters of Jerusalem, Cameron and Suzanne, and those they would call sister, work and weep in the present, and find deep joy as well, and await the outcome in the shadow of a hope that cannot yet fully be spoken.

NOTES

1. The phrase is a modification of a song title by Chris Williamson.
2. Maggie Kulyk interview with parishioner, 13 October 1992.
3. Simone de Beauvoir, *The Second Sex,* trans. H. M. Parshley (New York: Vintage Books, 1952). First published in France in 1949.
4. See Edith Wyschogrod's excellent summary of Heidegger's critique of the "logic of science" and its domination of Western philosophy in *Saints and Postmodernism: Revisioning Moral Philosophy* (Chicago: University of Chicago Press, 1990), especially chapter 5. See also the now classic essays in Hester Eisenstein and Alice Jardine, eds., *The Future of Difference* (New Brunswick, N.J.: Rutgers University Press, 1980). For a more contemporary development of "difference" as a category of analysis see Iris Marion Young, *Justice and the Politics of Difference* (Princeton, N.J.: Princeton University Press, 1990). In gay and lesbian studies, a good anthology is Diana Fuss, ed., *Inside/Out: Lesbian Theories, Gay Theories* (New York: Routledge, 1991).
5. bell hooks, *Feminist Theory: From Margin to Center* (Boston: South End Press, 1984).
6. Marginal groups are often competitive, as well, for the "remainder" of the scarce social goods available to those on the margins. Horizontal violence within and among disadvantaged communities is a constant.
7. I am being deliberately vague and general. My claims are based

on notes full of concrete examples the pastors shared with us, but which seem inappropriate to recount in detail.

8. Edward C. Lehman, Jr., *Women Clergy in England: Sexism, Modern Consciousness and Church Viability*, vol. 16 of *Studies in Religion and Society* (Lewiston, N.Y.: The Edwin Mellen Press, 1987). The last chapter of this book compares his findings among English groups with earlier research in the U.S.: Edward C. Lehman, Jr., *Women Clergy: Breaking Through Gender Barriers* (New Brunswick, N.J.: Transaction Publishers, 1985).

9. See, for example, Jackson W. Carroll, Barbara Hargrove, and Adair T. Lummis, *Women of the Cloth: A New Opportunity for the Churches* (San Francisco: Harper & Row, 1982); Thomas Beck Handley, *Congregational Leaders' Perception of the Pastoral Role: An Analysis of the Acceptance of Women Pastors* (Ann Arbor, Mich.: U.M.I., 1985); Catherine M. Prelinger, ed., *Episcopal Women: Gender, Spirituality, and Commitment in an American Mainline Denomination* (Oxford: Oxford University Press, 1992). The anecdotal evidence is immense.

10. In addition to the Fuss anthology and the work of Judith Butler already cited, see Michel Foucault, *The History of Sexuality, Volume I: An Introduction*, trans. Alan Sheridan (New York: Vintage Books, 1980) and the fascinating, disturbing biography of Foucault by James Miller, *The Passion of Michel Foucault* (New York: Simon and Schuster, 1993); Mandy Merck, *Perversions: Deviant Readings by Mandy Merck* (New York: Routledge, 1993); Eve Kosofsky Sedgwick, *Epistemology of the Closet* (Berkeley, Calif.: University of California Press, 1990). See also the film *Paris Is Burning*. Jennie Livingston (producer), *Paris Is Burning*, 1991. Distributed by Academy Entertainment, catalog no. 1495.

11. Susan Bordo, *Unbearable Weight: Feminism, Western Culture and the Body* (Berkeley, Calif.: University of California Press, 1993), 299.

12. See Rebecca S. Chopp, *The Power to Speak: Feminism, Language, God* (New York: Crossroad, 1989).

7 Some Modest Conclusions

One study of two churches cannot support a general theory of anything; this disclaimer bears repeating here. We cannot conclude anything in general about women clergy or about churches who hire women clergy or about how churches and their women clergy will understand and negotiate issues of power and authority. Different churches and different women clergy will tell different stories. On the other hand, we have been able to articulate some important conclusions about the two churches we studied. It is a feminist conviction that general theories somehow must be based upon narratives of real people's real lives in any case. Thus, the narratives of these two churches have the status of conversation partners in the ongoing development of American congregational research, gender studies, and Christian feminist ethics.

Our first observation was that the women clergy we studied do not embody a style or constellation of styles that have come to be known in the literature as women's ways of leadership. Furthermore, in their particular situations, each different from the other, the forcefulness and directiveness of their personal leadership and their astute maneuvering in the traditional arenas of church politics constitute important aspects of their effectiveness. They are outstanding women, that is, excellent beyond what is expected of their gender, and that fact was important in their being hired by the churches and in their contributions to their communities.

On the other hand, both women clergy embody qualities that their cultures associate with females, except those that would render them nonassertive leaders. To call on the familiar stereotypes, let me say that both women are feminine, and they dress and talk and behave in ways that are expected and familiar and unremarkable in their cultural settings.

All this leads to our discovery of the fluidity of gender as an analytical category.[1] As I noted in chapter 1, we had taken some care to identify churches for this study that were similar regarding some key sociological markers. We expected that gender would be constructed similarly in both congregations, that it would, as it were, hold still for us while we looked at other issues. What we found was that even in middle- to upper-middle-class, white Protestant churches in Atlanta, Georgia, gender was a very slippery concept and could not be a dependable point of comparison even in this very small, very limited group. Gender as we observed it can best be characterized as a set of expectations for how male persons and female persons will be. Those expectations turn out to intersect with so many other cultural factors that a woman at St. Matthew's could well experience her gender somewhat different from the way a woman at Bethany might. Furthermore, gender as a set of cultural expectations is also always a negotiation, a dynamic, relational reality, so that the individual characteristics of every woman will interact in somewhat different ways with social expectations, thereby reinscribing or reinterpreting them in very complex ways. That is, persons move about their worlds with some more or less clear expectations about how gender will function, look, and be. Any large, complex culture such as the one that characterizes the United States of America at the end of the twentieth century has uncounted smaller cultures, and within those, other smaller cultures.[2] Many persons in fact participate in and are shaped by many of these smaller cultures with similar or different or overlapping gender expectations. As persons interact, so do those expectations. Thus a person's gender will be a more or less prominent feature of his or her personhood in different settings with those different expectations and may, in fact, be experienced differently. Imagine, for example, what it is like to be a white middle-aged woman who is the only student in a physics class in a prominent undergraduate college, or to be that same person working alongside migrant farm workers, or to be that same person brought unidentified in an ambulance to a county hospital. Now change the race of the woman. Play with different combinations of age and wealth and race. We had assumed that female would be constructed more or less identically in the two churches and with regard to the role of senior clergy occupied by the two women in our study. What we found was that a female priest is a somewhat different creature than a female pastor due to the differences in the theologies of ordination and the understandings and enactments the two traditions have of priestly or pastoral authority. Before getting to know the two churches, we had assumed that their social and economic locations in Atlanta were similar enough that understandings of gender would not be affected. What we found, and have seen repeatedly in the accounts above, is that even with the relatively small demographic and economic differences between the churches, expectations and experiences regarding gender diverged in some important ways. Not least of these was the contrast between Bethany's assignment of many church tasks without regard for gender as opposed to St. Matthew's more clearly defined separation of those tasks. The contrast is not absolute; Bethany has not completely done away with gender roles, and St. Matthew's does not entirely adhere to conventional ones. Still, the contrast is easily observable. And that contrast regarding assignment of roles according to gender is analogous to, if not caused by, the demographic realities that church members do not leave at the door when they enter. Each church unsurprisingly reflects the social practices of its members. What surprised us was how deeply gender was implicated in the differences. Even under the relatively controlled, restricted terms of our study, gender simply would not hold still either as an experiential or end analytical category.

What we found in the case of these two clergywomen and their churches was precisely the dynamic of expanding gender expectations. These conventionally female women lead in ways that are not necessarily associated with being female, and in both congregations, gender expectations are being broadened. In the case of Bethany, gender division was already less rigid than at St. Matthew's, and that may continue to be the case for some time based upon the different demographic makeup of the two congregations. On the other hand, Suzanne's presence at St. Matthew's may begin to pry open some of the closed places in that social segment's understanding of what is possible regarding allocation of gender roles in ways that group does not encounter elsewhere. Unlike other small cultures in our time and place, these two groups still contained persons and subgroups whose expectations for gender and leadership did not resemble the leaders they now have. Pockets of resentment, experiences of surprise, even expressions of betrayal preceded the settled trust and confidence that now characterize both churches' experiences of their leaders.

The gender of the senior clergy ceased being an issue when it ceased running up against expectations that there was something odd about what was going on. We saw the transition much more clearly at St. Matthew's than at Bethany because of Suzanne's relatively short tenure at St. Matthew's when our research began. One St. Matthew's member expressed well the general sense we heard many times, and heard as fading memory from Bethany members.

This woman was initially unhappy about the church's decision to call a woman, but she soon changed her mind. Remarking about Suzanne, she said, "She came with such a gracious attitude, and her preaching was good, and she was obviously very conscientious about it, that I forget that she is a woman, for whatever that is worth."[3] From our perspective, it is worth a very great deal. The taken-for-granted nature of these women senior clergy is, of course, part of the expansion of gender expectations themselves. As I argued in the last chapter, the women themselves do not radically challenge a wide range of gender expectations, and that fact enabled the smooth transition to their leadership that both churches experienced. As we saw in the narratives of the churches, both women are the right kind of women for their congregations. A St. Matthew's member told us that while Suzanne's dynamic leadership was fine, they could not have handled what she imagined would be a more abrasive style if the pastor were from "the north."[4] Suzanne is forceful, and she is southern. As we have seen, both clergywomen are firmly anchored in and represent their denomination's traditions. Cameron and Suzanne fulfilled regional and denominational expectations; they remained conventional women for their settings at the same time that they provided the kind of dynamic, forceful, directive, and politically skilled leadership that some might associate more directly with a male style. And the combination of conventional gender behavior and forceful leadership itself contributed significantly to the transformation of gender expectations and stereotypes that remain. Both women encounter continued pockets of resentment and surprise and both continue to counter them with continued effective leadership.

Another version of our disclaimer regarding generalizability: The experience of these two churches cannot be generalized to the experience of churches who hire female clergy. From other sources and experiences we know, for example, that conventional gender embodiment is not a necessary criterion for effective leadership. We know that what counts as conventional gender embodiment is a contextual and relational issue and will vary from place to place. We know that forceful, directive leadership is not the only effective style for men or women. In this case, what we found was that the transformation of gender expectations could take place even when the embodiment of those expectations was largely, and not entirely, conventional.

We can say with certainty that the two churches in this study have not compromised the care and leadership of their congregations by their decision to hire women in their senior clergy position. The costs of the decision, rather, have been borne by the women themselves who have in the past suffered, and continue to suffer, from expectations that their gender and their vocation are somehow in conflict. They know better, their churches know better, we know better; and it is our hope that their experiences and that of their congregations will reduce the painful consequences of being a strong, forceful, and effective female clergywoman for those who are sure to follow.

NOTES

1. In what follows, I will be talking only about females, since that is the gender we studied. Our general findings regarding the fluid, relational nature of gender may apply to men as well, but that would be a topic for another study. It is also possible that the two genders are not symmetrical and/or analogical with regard to the observations being made here.
2. It is, of course, arguable that the U.S.A. now has no culture as such. For the sake of this conversation, I am assuming that the total of all cultural expressions that exist in this time and place constitutes a complex, changing, yet recognizably North American culture that provides a loose common context for our lives.
3. Maggie Kulyk interview with a parishioner, 17 February 1993.
4. Maggie Kulyk interview with a parishioner, October 1992.

Works Cited

de Beauvoir, Simone. *The Second Sex.* Trans. H. M. Parshley. New York: Vintage Books, 1952.

Belenky, Mary Field, Blythe McVicker Clinchy, Nancy Rule Goldberger, and Jill Mattuck Tarule, eds. *Women's Ways of Knowing: The Development of Self, Voice and Mind.* New York: Basic Books, 1986.

Bordo, Susan. *Unbearable Weight: Feminism, Western Culture and the Body.* Berkeley, Calif.: University of California Press, 1993.

Brownmiller, Susan. *Femininity.* New York: Simon and Schuster, 1984.

Butler, Judith, and Joan W. Scott, eds. *Feminists Theorize the Political.* New York: Routledge, 1992.

Butler, Judith. *Gender Trouble: Feminism and the Subversion of Identity.* New York: Routledge, 1990.

———. *Bodies that Matter: On the Discursive Limits of Sex.* New York: Routledge, 1993.

Cannon, Katie. *Black Womanist Ethics.* Atlanta: Scholars Press, 1988.

Cannon, Katie, Ada Maria Isasi-Diaz, Kwok Pui-lan, and Letty M. Russell, eds. *Inheriting Our Mother's Gardens: Feminist Theology in Third World Perspective.* Philadelphia: Westminster Press, 1988.

Carr, Anne. *Transforming Grace: Christian Tradition and Women's Experience.* San Francisco: Harper & Row, 1988.

Carroll, Jackson, Carl S. Dudley, and William McKinney, eds. *Handbook for Congregational Studies.* Nashville: Abingdon Press, 1989.

Carroll, Jackson, Barbara Hargrove, and Adair T. Lummis. *Women of the Cloth: A New Opportunity for Churches.* San Francisco: Harper & Row, 1982.

Chopp, Rebecca S. *The Power to Speak: Feminism, Language and God.* New York: Crossroad, 1989.

Christ, Carol, and Judith Plaskow, eds. *Womanspirit Rising: A Feminist Reader in Religion.* San Francisco: Harper & Row, 1979.

Collins, Patricia Hill. *Black Feminist Thought: Knowledge, Consciousness and the Politics of Empowerment.* New York: Routledge, 1990.

Diamond, Irene, and Lee Quinby, eds. *Feminism and Foucault: Reflections on Resistance.* Boston: Northeastern University Press, 1988.

Donovan, Mary Sudman. *A Different Call: Women's Ministries in the Episcopal Church, 1850–1920*. Wilton, Conn.: Morehouse-Barlow, 1986.

Dudley, Carl S., Jackson Carroll, and James. P. Wind, eds. *Carriers of Faith: Lessons from Congregational Studies*. Louisville, Ky.: Westminster John Knox Press, 1991.

Eisenstein, Hester, and Alice Jardine, eds. *The Future of Difference*. New Brunswick, N.J.: Rutgers University Press, 1980.

The Episcopal Church. *Constitution and Canons for the Government of the Protestant Episcopal Church in the United States of America Otherwise Known as the Episcopal Church*. The General Conventions, 1991.

Farley, Margaret. "Feminist Ethics." In *The Westminster Dictionary of Christian Ethics,* ed. James F. Childress and John Macquarrie. Philadephia: Westminster Press, 1986.

Foucault, Michel. *The History of Sexuality, Volume I: An Introduction*. Trans. Alan Sheridan. New York: Vintage Books, 1980.

Frank, Tom. *Vital Congregations—Faithful Disciples: Vision for the Church*. Foundational Document of the United Methodist Council of Bishops. Nashville: Graded Press, 1990.

Fraser, Nancy. *Unruly Practices: Power, Discourse and Gender in Contemporary Social Theory*. Minneapolis: University of Minnesota Press, 1989.

Fuss, Diana, ed. *Inside/Out: Lesbian Theories, Gay Theories*. New York: Routledge, 1991.

Gilligan, Carol. *In a Different Voice: Psychological Theory and Women's Development*. Cambridge, Mass.: Harvard University Press, 1982.

Gornick, Vivian, and Barbara K. Moral, eds. *Woman in Sexist Society: Studies in Power and Powerlessness*. New York: Basic Books, 1971.

Hahn, Celia Allison. *Sexual Paradox: Creative Tensions in Our Lives and in Our Congregations*. New York: Pilgrim Press, 1991.

Handley, Thomas Beck. *Congregational Leaders' Perception of the Pastoral Role: An Analysis of the Acceptance of Women Pastors*. Ann Arbor, Mich.: U.M.I., 1985.

Haraway, Donna. *Simians, Cyborgs and Women: The Reinvention of Nature*. New York: Routledge, 1991.

Helgesen, Sally. *The Female Advantage: Women's Ways of Leadership*. New York: Doubleday, 1990.

Hunter College Women's Collective. *Women's Realities, Women's Choices*. New York: Oxford University Press, 1983.

Heyward, Carter. *Touching Our Strength: The Erotic as Power and the Love of God*. San Francisco: Harper & Row, 1989.

hooks, bell. *Feminist Theory: From Margin to Center*. Boston: South End Press, 1984.

———. *Talking Back: Thinking Feminist/Thinking Black*. Boston: South End Press, 1989.

———. *Yearning: Race, Gender and Cultural Politics*. Boston: South End Press, 1990.

Janeway, Elizabeth. *Powers of the Weak*. New York: Knopf, 1980.

Johnson, Cathryn. "Gender and Formal Authority." *Social Psychology Quarterly* 56, no. 3 (1993): 193–210.

———. "Gender and Legitimate Authority." *American Sociological Review* 59 (February 1994): 122–135.

Lakoff, Robin Tolmach. *Talking Power: The Politics of Language in Our Lives.* New York: Basic Books, 1990.

Lehman, Edward C., Jr. *Women Clergy: Breaking Through Gender Barriers.* New Brunswick, N.J.: Transaction Publishers, 1985.

———. *Women Clergy in England: Sexism, Modern Consciousness and Church Viability.* Vol. 16 of *Studies in Religion and Society.* Lewiston, N.Y.: The Edwin Mellon Press, 1987.

Lorde, Audre. *Sister/Outsider.* Trumansburg, N.Y.: The Crossing Press, 1984.

Marrett, Michael McFarlene. *The Lambeth Conferences and Women Priests: The Historical Background of the Conferences and Their Impact on the Episcopal Church in America.* Smithtown, N.Y.: Exposition Press, 1981.

Merck, Mandy. *Perversions: Deviant Readings by Mandy Merck.* New York: Routledge, 1993.

Miller, James. *The Passion of Michel Foucault.* New York: Simon and Schuster, 1993.

Morrison, Toni, ed. *Race-ing Justice, En-gendering Power: Essays on Anita Hill, Clarence Thomas, and the Construction of Social Reality.* New York: Pantheon Books, 1992.

Nagel, Thomas. *The View from Nowhere.* New York: Oxford University Press, 1986.

Poling, James. *The Abuse of Power: A Theological Problem.* Nashville: Abingdon Press, 1991.

Prelinger, Catherine, ed. *Episcopal Women: Gender, Spirituality, and Commitment in an American Mainline Denomination.* Oxford: Oxford University Press, 1992.

Purvis, Sally B. *The Power of the Cross: Foundations for a Feminist Ethic of Community.* Nashville: Abingdon Press, 1993.

Rhodes, Lynn. *Co-Creating: A Feminist Vision of Ministry.* Philadelphia: Westminster Press, 1987.

Ruether, Rosemary Radford. *Sexism and God-Talk: Toward a Feminist Theology.* Boston: Beacon Press, 1983.

Russell, Letty M., ed. *The Church with Aids.* Louisville, Ky.: Westminster John Knox Press, 1990.

———. *Household of Freedom: Authority in Feminist Theology.* Philadelphia: Westminster, Press, 1987.

———. *Church in the Round: Feminist Interpretation of the Church.* Louisville, Ky.: Westminster John Knox Press, 1993.

Sawicki, Jana. *Disciplining Foucault: Feminism, Power, and the Body.* New York: Routledge, 1991.

Sedgwick, Eve Kosofshy. *Epistemology of the Closet.* Berkeley, Calif.: University of California Press, 1990.

Sennett, Richard. *Authority*. New York: Knopf, 1980.

Thistlethwaite, Susan. *Sex, Race and God: Christian Feminism in Black and White*. New York: Crossroad, 1989.

Townes, Emilie M. *Womanist Justice, Womanist Hope*. Atlanta: Scholars Press, 1993.

———. ed. *A Troubling in My Soul: Womanist Perspectives on Evil and Suffering*. Maryknoll, N.Y.: Orbis Books, 1993.

Weedon, Chris. *Feminist Practice and Poststructuralist Theory*. London: Basil Blackwell, 1987.

Welsh, Sharon D. *A Feminist Ethic of Risk*. Minneapolis: Fortress Press, 1990.

Williams, Delores. *Sisters in the Wilderness: The Challenge of Womanist God-Talk*. Maryknoll, N.Y.: Orbis Books, 1993.

Wind, James P. *Places of Worship: Exploring Their History*. Nashville: American Association for State and Local History, 1990.

———. "Leading Congregations, Discovering Congregational Culture," *Christian Century*, (February 3–10, 1993): 105–14.

Wyschogrod, Edith. *Saints and Postmodernism: Revisioning Moral Philosophy*. Chicago: University of Chicago Press, 1990.

Young, Iris Marion. *Justice and the Politics of Difference*. Princeton, N.J.: Princeton University Press, 1990.

———. *Throwing like a Girl and Other Essays in Feminist Philosophy and Social Theory*. Bloomington, Ind.: Indiana University Press, 1990.

Zelditch, Morris, Jr., and Henry A. Walker. *Advances in Group Processes*. Vol 1. New York: J.A.I Press, 1984.